MOVIETONE PRESENTS THE TWENTIETH CENTURY

MOVIETONE PRESENTS THE TWENTIETH CENTURY

Lawrence Cohn

ANDRE DEUTSCH

This book is presented as a tribute to the unselfish dedication and daring of the worldwide staff of Movietonews, Inc., past as well as present.

First published in 1977 by André Deutsch Limited
105 Great Russell Street, London WC1
Copyright © 1976 by Lawrence Cohn
All rights reserved
ISBN 233968822
Printed in the United States of America

THOSE THRILLING MOVIETONE DAYS AND NIGHTS

by Lowell Thomas

These photographs are from the newsreels that we saw at the movies before the advent of television, some even before radio. The personalities are politicians, celebrities, some merely notorious, men and women like ourselves, who gave the 1920's, '30's, '40's and '50's their energy, their grim times, their happy times, and their character, too. Here's history as the world saw it, how it looked to us who made the newsreels. These rare pictures are from our archives. I was the voice of Movietone and one of its editors for two decades and I am going to try and give you an idea of what the newsreel was all about.

My own film career got its first impetus in 1914 and '15 on expeditions to Alaska and the Yukon, and even more so when I set out with a cameraman to make a record of World War I in 1917 and '18. When we first went off to capture war events, we found our equipment bulky, hard to manage; also commanders were reluctant to let our cameramen risk their lives for a front line news story. Film crews turned to a practice that was rather common before the war and was used again and again in later years. Some battle scenes and other exciting events were staged and then presented as reality. But they were authentic, unforgettable, and did provide the excitement cameramen felt was needed for the newsreel.

Less than a year later the young Fox Film Company offered its first newsreel issue and its idealistic tone was set by a foreword. (The early newsreel actually was for prestige rather than profit.) A letter came from President Wilson, and in launching what was to be the most important and longest-lived of all the newsreels he said: "I'm interested and deeply gratified to learn that the Fox Company is intending to devote its news-weekly to the promotion of universal and lasting peace. It can render the greatest service. The motion picture industry as an educator and as a power for good can be made of the greatest service to the nation and to the world and I congratulate the company on its public-spirited plan."

Movietone consistently came through with the best newsreel coverage, right around the world. From the first issue our cameramen and representatives were in some thirty international locations, even in Northern Russia. By 1922 more than a thousand Fox newspeople were cranking cameras from Hollywood to the African jungle and the Australian Outback. The idea was to have a man within a few hours travelling distance of significant events. For instance our cameramen rushed to Sicily and got Mount Etna in wild eruption. Luckily the volcano took its time, but the film proved that on short notice our cameras could be almost anywhere. Between assignments, part-time correspondents were filming travelogues and shorts of all sorts. Later it was a Fox newsreel cameraman on a travel film assignment in Hawaii who got the Movietone exclusive footage of the bombing of Pearl Harbor.

As older readers will recall, all early newsreels were silent. Apart from some experimenting, sound movies were still way out in the future. Captions identified and explained all the scenes.

To rush film to theaters as soon as election results were known, Movietone prepared scenes in advance, using old newsreel pictures of candidates, all film available from our newsreel library. For instance, we were all set to announce the victory of John W. Davis over McAdoo and Al Smith, with one version ready in case of an election deadlock that would have thrown the decision into the House of Representatives. Actually every theater had three of our versions ready to run, and we always were well ahead of our competition.

In May 1927, Movietone became the first newsreel to use sound, and our cameramen at once set off around the world. Compared to the campaign coverage of silent days, sound newsreels made new demands on politicians whose style previously had been geared to street corners and convention crowds. The intimacy of the sound camera quickly resulted in a new political speaking style. Franklin Delano Roosevelt and his advisers were among the first to grasp the importance of sound newsreels, how to use them to shape public opinion. His closeups, looking right through the lens at the people of the United States, were startlingly effective. F. D. R. was quite a showman!

Sound trucks were built and rushed into the field. Japan attacked China, and Movietone filmed the fall of Shanghai. In 1936, when civil war broke out in Spain, Movietone sent eleven sound film crews to record action on both sides. Here, and in the war years ahead, the newsreel kept its pledge to bring history home to us, history in the making.

The main idea behind newsreel coverage of course was to enable the invisible audience to get a glimpse of events as they happened. Ah, but there was a temptation. News events *sometimes* were actually created, stirred-up by the newsreel crews. So some news events did give us a rather limited point of view. Rarely were the views of social and intellectual minorities well covered. Newsreel cameramen and audiences alike knew that the easiest way to get coverage was to have things pre-planned—for instance, pomp and circumstance ceremonies often were arranged with the camera in mind.

Twice weekly our reels were put together at high speed under much pressure. Stories and episodes would be chosen, edited, text written, and music and sound effects added. All this we did in long sleepless night sessions and then our reels were rushed out to the theaters.

We were indeed eyewitnesses to much history. But when we didn't have new scenes to illustrate important stories, sometimes we would re-edit similar scenes, add new information to the sound track and so on. Sometimes we even missed an event and had to improvise.

For forty-five years our Fox Movietone News cameramen were almost everywhere, nearly always getting great film. For some five thousand newsreels, our cameramen, film editors, writers, and commentators recorded events and happenings right around the globe. Even if the news wasn't particularly interesting, we'd try to make it that way. This book gives us a chance to look back into those fabulous Movietone archives, those twenty some years when, twice a week, we worked frantically through the night so you might be informed and entertained.

THE MOVIETONE STORY

Though perhaps difficult to imagine today, there was a time in the not-too-distant past when no movie program was complete without a newsreel. Before the onslaught of television, the standard movie theater program was comprised of two features, previews of coming attractions, possibly a short-subject and/or a cartoon and *always,* the newsreel. With the advent of the newsreel, all of the activities of 20th Century man were presented visually via the medium of the motion picture. The subjects covered were all-encompassing: politics and politicians of the day, kings and king-makers, dictators and demagogues, sports, transportation, technology, science, disasters, conflagrations, news events, not-so-newsworthy events, persons and personalities, planes and trains, fashions of the day and of yesterday. Fads and follies, crazes and crazies, the interesting as well as the banal, public works, some entertainment, and always, war — the last being *the* constant item throughout both the history of newsreels and apparently, the behavior of modern man.

Movietone News had its inception in 1919 as Fox News. This was in the silent, pre-sound days, and the first theatrical issue was premiered in New York City on October 11, 1919. From the very beginning and throughout the sound-era to its final presentation of October 1, 1963, when Movietone News ceased operations in the United States as an active producer of newsreel programs (and became an archival operation), there were two newsreels issued each and every week as well as additional "specials." These latter supplements were of extraordinary events such as the Japanese sneak attack on Pearl Harbor, the Hindenburg disaster, and the joint assassination of the King of Yugoslavia and the Prime Minister of France in 1934. The "specials" were generally full-length newsreels presented to the subscribing movie theaters as a public service, at no extra charge. Thus between the years 1919 and 1963, approximately 5,000 newsreel programs were presented theatrically in this country by Movietone News. In order to assemble this extraordinary historical record, over 100 million feet of film was shot throughout the world, with approximately 7 million being used in the final assemblages. The Fox Newsreel, founded by William Fox, was the last of the major newsreels to commence operation. But despite this fact, it expanded rapidly and very shortly thereafter outdistanced all other competitors. From its inception, Fox had extensive coverage throughout the world, with staff cameramen and overseas representation in Yokohama, Tokyo, Shanghai, Peking, Hong Kong, Canton, Manila, Honolulu, Wellington, New Zealand, Sydney, Melbourne, New Guinea, Borneo, Sumatra, Tibet, Siberia, Irkutsk, Manchuria, Alaska, Stockholm, Dublin, Liverpool, London, Copenhagen, La Havre, Paris, Bordeaux, Brussels, Lisbon, Madrid, and Rome—as well as throughout the United States, Canada and South America. Additionally, production centers were formed in Great Britain, France, Germany, and Australia. These production offices operated independently under the guidance of the New York home office, the result being a virtually constant flow of material dispersed to theaters throughout the world. More than 1,000 cameramen were employed, either on staff or as freelancers, and the camera crews and editorial staffs recorded in film and sound the history and happenings of the twentieth century.

Movietone News (Fox News) employed a number of mottos during its existence: "Mightiest of All," "Around the World in Fifteen Minutes in Picture and Sound," "It Speaks for Itself," and "It Speaks for Itself in Any Language" were the most widely used. Additionally, the newsreel (at its height) was made in approximately 47 languages for over 50 different countries. Some of the languages were Hungarian, Arabic, Portuguese, Polish, Italian, German, Russian, Swiss, Flemish, Dutch, Swedish, French, Czech, German, South African (2 versions: English and Afrikanner) English-English, American-English, and numerous others. The complete list of countries was as follows:

Argentina	Estonia	Peru
Australia	Finland	Philippines
Austria	France	Portugal
Belgium	Germany	Puerto Rico
Brazil	Greece	Roumania
Bulgaria	Holland	Salvador
Canada	Hungary	Scotland
Chile	India	South Africa
China	Indo-China	Sweden
Colombia	Irish Free State	Switzerland
Cuba	Japan	Syria
Czechoslovakia	Latvia	Turkey
Denmark	Mexico	United States
Dutch East Indies	New Zealand	Uruguay
Ecuador	Northern Ireland	Venezuela
Egypt	Norway	Wales
England	Panama	Yugoslavia

Thus it can be seen that as a practical matter, the entire world was covered by Movietone, both geographically and by language. And similarly, nearly every aspect of human life and change was recorded. The early days were replete with adventure and daredevil tactics by the Fox cameramen, who stopped at nothing, not only to secure a story but, competitively, to "scoop" the other newsreel companies. In the process, they risked their lives daily in order to get exciting footage.

In 1927 the Fox-Case Corp. was formed, in addition to Fox News. Theodore Case, head of the new operation, was a sound engineer who was involved with Earl Sponable, the man acknowledged to be the genius of developing and refining the sound-on-film technique. Fox-Case was short-lived, lasting about two years, and dealt primarily with very special events and short-duration (approximately 15 minutes) entertainment pieces. The latter included segments with famed humorist Robert Benchley and items such as George Gershwin rehearsing a show and playing the piano. Fox-Case's first news special was the take-off of Charles Lindbergh's famous trans-Atlantic, non-stop flight to Paris in 1927. This event was also one of the very first attempts at sound-on-film by a newsreel. By 1926 Fox News had become Fox-Movietone News, and in 1931 it became 20th Century-Fox Movietone News, by which designation it was known until its demise (as a producer) in 1963. (Although the official corporate name was "Movietonews," the company was always referred to as "Movietone News.")

To complete this brief genealogy, mention should be made of two other "associations." The first was around 1930-1934 and involved Hearst Metrotone News. During this period of time the Hearst Corporation was using Fox sound equipment, such items being at a premium, and in order for both organizations to save money during the Depression years, the same footage was shot and shared by both. However, each company still maintained its own organization, staff, and editors. The result was that although the combination of filming efforts saved money, the resulting stories were not necessarily the same, each having been edited to reflect the particular point of view of the parent company.

The second association was with United Press International and lasted eleven years, from 1952 to 1963. This joint effort formed a world-wide television news service, and it was afforded on a daily basis to independent television stations who were not affiliated with networks. They supplied approximately 110 stations in the U.S. alone, and maintained a staff of eight to ten writers in New York City, plus a slightly smaller complement in Washington, D.C.; between the two cities the yield was fifteen or more stories per day. Eventually the operation began to lose money and the association was discontinued.

It has been suggested that the initial silent newsreels were giveaways to the motion picture theaters, but that attitude remained only until it was realized that the newsreels were not only popular and entertaining, but were also potentially an extremely profitable item. Although the early silent presentations generally dealt with subjects of little consequence, they did afford the public an opportunity to view, very shortly after the event occurred, that which was (subjectively) considered to be news of the day.

In addition to the relatively inconsequential subject matter presented, many of the early newsreels were staged and combined some actual footage with the magical additions and interspersing of film shot in Hollywood (or elsewhere). Thus an infantry charge during World War I might have been filmed on a field in New Jersey rather than in Europe, a ship disaster would be an amalgam of the actual footage plus Hollywood stunt-men in the "act" of abandoning ship. And even though the newsreel process became more sophisticated as the years passed, this device was still employed, although to a lesser extent. Staged arrests of smugglers and bootleggers took place during prohibition days, and even later, during the dust-bowl Depression days, staged coverage was presented of an "authentic" mass-migration of "Okies" from the Southwest to California and of the subsequent refusal of entry by "authorities" at the state line. Despite this, the newsreels afforded an immediacy, an instant opportunity to view history as it occurred, as well as the additional opportunity to be educated, informed, and entertained all at the same time.

Being silent, the original Fox Newsreels were presented with titles and were 10 to 15 minutes in length. As previously mentioned, they could best be described as inconsequential or perhaps even trivial. But, the audiences were able to *see* world figures, celebrities, and the various and varied events of the day, and this was, of course, not the case with newspapers or fledgling radio.

In those heroic silent days Fox cameramen hauled about equipment that weighed, in the aggregate, over half a ton. And despite this bulk and unwieldiness, as well as the relatively unsophisticated quality of the results, they managed to present coverage of national and international events on a continuing, professional basis. These early cameramen were daredevils in the most literal, adventuresome sense. The images presented are those of men dragging massive photographic equipment up the skeletal structure of the George Washington Bridge, or that of the Chrysler Building, or over the resplendent oval dome of a church in Rome. They flew over the mouth of the erupting volcano Mt. Vesuvius and were passengers in early bi-planes of questionable flying capabilities in order to film the monstrous Graf Zeppelin in flight. It is indeed difficult to imagine this being done at all, let alone under the burdensome and dangerous circumstances described. However, these men were obsessively driven, much as the "Front Page" reporters of the era: anything, even to the extent of endangering one's life, to achieve the all-important *story*.

With the advent of sound-on-film in 1927 things became a bit more complicated technically. Movietone was the first newsreel to use this technique, and was also the first company to use "portable," single-system lightweight cameras and recording equipment. This innovation resulted in the reduction of the total weight to 300 pounds and in the process added immeasurably to the ease of mobility which was so essential to the filming of news events. By this time, Movietone was well ahead of its competitors, an enviable position it was to maintain until the end, and its personnel, resources, overseas representation and syndication (more than 3,000 movie theaters in the U.S. alone) exceeded all of the other newsreel companies combined.

Sound newsreels also resulted in a slightly more complex approach to editing (synchronization and sound levels being two of the problems that bore no consideration in the silent days). Schooling was afforded both cameramen and editors to teach them the techniques of the new approach. The early sound newsreels were, in retrospect, exceedingly dull; the "natural" sound of traffic noises, people crossing the street, the sounds made by a newly hatched bird, as well as the tumult, shouting and engine noises of a major news story such as Lindbergh's take-off were some of the initial, early efforts. Not very discriminating perhaps, but this was the dawning of the sound era and looked at in the light of the time period, sound for sound's sake alone was an exceptionally exciting event. Initially, virtually all that was presented was "natural" sound with very little, if any, commentary. Then around 1934 producer Truman Talley, a former newspaperman from *The New York Times* and a man of extraordinary vision, initiated the era of commentator personalities. Some of these men have since become synonomous with and inseparable from Movietone News and the genre of news reporting in general. Lowell Thomas, Ed Thorgersen, Mel Allen, Paul Douglas and resident zany, Lew "Monkies Is the Cwaziest People" Lehr, received extraordinarily widespread popularity, and it is safe to say that their voices and images were among the most widely known in the United States. (And, of course, the various non-American Movietone companies had their equivalent counterparts in popularity.)

In the final analysis, the sound-on-film process, along with the commentator approach, changed the face of news reporting for all time, and even today, years after the height of popularity of the newsreel in this country, the television approach to news reporting is primarily based upon the techniques, systems, and approaches developed by the newsreel.

PRODUCING THE NEWSREELS

Movietone News was totally housed in a single, self-contained facility at 460 West 54th Street in New York City. The building had 4 floors and was physically set up as follows: *First Floor*—complete sound stages, employed for the production of fashion stories and short-subjects as well as being utilized for screen-tests for 20th Century-Fox Film Co. aspirants and production of feature films. The stages were fully equipped, even including a small swimming pool for underwater shots, and in many instances sets were constructed to specifically accommodate the subject matter being filmed.

Second Floor—short-subjects. Movietone filmed several hundred short featurettes at the rate of approximately 26 per year. They dealt with many diverse subjects—music, travel, transportation, adventure, technology, sports, urban and rural American life, etc., and were sold to the theaters along with Fox feature films and the newsreels. The short-subjects department maintained a staff separate from the news division with their own cameramen and cutting-staff and on many occasions made up special stories incorporating regular newsreel footage. The 20th Century-Fox research laboratory was also located there.

Third Floor—Movietone News. This floor housed the entire news department: cameramen, commentators, editors, contact men *et. al.,* and this is where the daily activities concerning newsreel production by Movietone took place.

Fourth Floor—Library. Here is where all of the newsreels, past as well as current, cut-stories (the actual newsreels as they appeared theatrically), and out-takes (those not used) were housed, as well as all index-cards, "dope" sheets (information reports filed with film footage by the cameramen, serving as supplements to the information recorded on the index-cards) and various cross-reference files arranged alphabetically, numerically, and by subject matter.

Mechanics of the Newsreel: A typical production operation would take the following form. The news editor, under instructions from the producer and/or the General Manager, assigned the stories to be covered and designated the cameramen. In the area of sports, stories were generally suggested and assigned by the sports editor. Contact-men would usually set up things in advance and would, additionally, take care of strictly routine and mechanical matters such as securing various permissions, necessary permits, admission tickets, etc., so that the actual filming process could proceed as efficiently and effectively as possible, with little in the way of surprises and without interference from outside sources. The department was open 24 hours a day, 7 days a week.

Wherever and whenever possible, the camera crews consisted of a cameraman, a soundman (once sound-on-film became available), and an assistant. After they shot the pictures, the negative was brought into the office. If a story was coming in from overseas, it generally came in developed rather than in negative form. The "make-up" days for the newsreel were on Mondays and Thursdays, and after the cameramen presented their film, it was sent to the laboratory for processing and was normally developed overnight. There were no work-prints made in those days, and a typical week would find the cutting-staff putting the negatives on reels for projection and viewing on Monday. At this time the make-up editor (chief film-cutter) would sit with the producer and the news editor and view the negative. The stories to be considered for the forthcoming newsreel would be decided upon, and editorial assignments would be made for a "rough cut" of the stories. In most cases a selection would be made of the best parts of the story, and a ten minute segment might be severely edited, resulting in perhaps two or three minutes of total playing time.

After the selecting, editing, and cutting were completed, the proposed stories were sent to the laboratory for black-and-white master prints, and eventually they would be sent to other major producing centers outside of the United States: England, France, Australia, and prior to World War II, Germany. One of the black-and-white master prints (sometimes called "lavenders" in the United States because of the tint, and "blueprints" in Europe) would be used for re-editing; a work-print would be made, and the negative, out-takes and the cut-negatives would be sent to the library for filing and archival storage. From this point on all work was done from the black-and-white master, rather than risking damage to or perhaps even destruction of the original negative.

The stories then received final editing and selection after being run many times subsequent to the work-print being assembled. A final choice would be made of seven or eight stories selected from an original number of perhaps two dozen. They were then shown to the commentators and text-writers, "calculations" were made showing the exact running time of each scene, and the texts were written. The black-and-white work-prints were matched for music, sound, and sound-effects on a separate track, in addition to the "natural" sound which was already present on the footage. Thereafter, everything went to the recording room, and the commentator went for a "take" of his commentary. When this was completed, all sound was combined on a single piece of film and a sound negative was made. The sound negative was sent to the laboratory to be developed, a positive was made, and the film master and sound-negative were matched. A dup (duplicate) was made, and the result was a dup negative with combined sound. Main titles, end titles, and dateline titles were then decided upon by the editors, and title-cards were printed and then filmed on positive film on a title-stand. Appropriate titles were superimposed upon a frame from one of the scenes to be presented and were interpolated into the master before the final duplicate was printed. The results, a completed sound track and picture, were run for the commentators and editors, sent out for final printing, and the newsreel was then ready for shipment to the subscribing theaters. Six-to seven-hundred newsreel prints were made for the East Coast alone, with additional prints being made in Chicago and Los Angeles. The various regions would also add or delete stories such as coverage of local football games, which would have regional interest but would not necessarily be of national importance or interest.

All of the foregoing would begin at 8:00 A.M. Monday and would be completed by 3:00 or 4:00 A.M. Tuesday. On Thursday the identical process would recommence at 8:00 A.M. The Movietone studio was a very busy, often frantic, place to work.

ON THE SCENE WITH MOVIETONE

During the varied and exciting Movietone years, there were countless events of varying degrees of importance that received coverage: the collapse of Honeymoon Bridge at Niagara Falls; Franklin D. Roosevelt declaring war against Japan; the Crown Prince of Germany in exile after World War I; the Scopes "Monkey" trial; Ku Klux Klan meetings; an important "special" release in several installments in 1922 entitled "Face to Face With Japan," which asked the question "Does war threaten between the United States and Japan?"; coverage of the Mexican bandit Pancho Villa; Charles Lindbergh's historic take-off and his landing in Paris; the Tokyo earthquake of 1924; interviews with Sir Arthur Conan Doyle, creator of Sherlock Holmes, as well as several with George Bernard Shaw; wartime events throughout the world—Germany, Italy, Ethiopia, Algeria and Japan; Hitler, Mussolini and myriad preparatory "arrangements" leading to the second World War; and a plethora of other topics such as strikes, civil disobedience, coronations, elections, fashions, and sporting events.

There were however some events which, by any standards, were of an extraordinary nature. Three of the most sensational, in every sense of the term, were the Hindenburg disaster (1937), the Japanese sneak attack on Pearl Harbor (1941), and the politically motivated assassinations of King Alexander I of Yugoslavia and Jean Louis Barthou, Prime Minister of France (1934). The coverage that each received comprises that of which legends are made.

A superb example of Movietone's on-the-spot coverage was the filming of the tragic Hindenburg disaster on a cloudy, overcast day at Lakehurst, New Jersey, on May 6, 1937. Undoubtedly one of the most dramatic newsreel events of all time, the explosion reduced the dirigible to a smoldering mass of ruins within seconds, and several members of the New York staff were directly under the huge airship when it exploded. The Hindenburg had made numerous Atlantic crossings, and the one of May 6th was expected to be no different from the many previous routine landings. Despite a history of nothing unusual happening, this symbol of Hitler's Nazi Germany was covered at every landing by Movietone cameramen because of Editor-in-Chief Truman Talley's intuitive feeling that someday the Hindenburg would explode. Therefore, despite the protests of the various camera crews, one was always present, and Talley's intuition resulted in the timely coverage of one of the most famous events of all time (by cameramen Al Gold, Larry Kennedy, and Deon De Titta, Jr. and sound engineer Addison Tice).

Although the Hindenburg disaster coverage was the result of planning based upon intuition, films of the Japanese sneak attack on Pearl Harbor were rather the result of happenstance. Cameraman Al Brick was in Hawaii shooting a documentary short-subject on the United States Navy called "Filming the Fleet," and because of this assignment was at Pearl Harbor on that eventful Sunday morning. Brick, the sole newsreel man there, photographed the entire assault and subsequent holocaust. His footage was immediately impounded by the government, was thereafter developed and censored after a military screening that included several Movietone executives. A censored version was released, with copies given by Movietone to the competitive newsreel companies, at the request of the government. Approximately one year later the uncensored, complete version of Pearl Harbor, incorporating Al Brick's footage, was released to the public.

One of the most significant, far-reaching, and spectacular political events of the 20th Century was the assassination on October 9, 1934, of King Alexander I of Yugoslavia and French Foreign Minister Jean Louis Barthou in Marseilles, France. The assassination occurred during a routine state visit by Alexander to France. It was to be, ostensibly, an ordinary event, one of many covered by brothers Georges and Raymond Mejat, two of the top cameramen in Europe. The brothers, who worked out of the Movietone office in Paris, drove a newly furnished sound truck to Marseilles and made the necessary preparations. Georges was to shoot the arrival of the King on his destroyer, and Raymond was to be stationed further along the parade route. Georges filmed the arrival and meeting of the King and the assembled dignitaries. Shortly thereafter, the motorcade through the streets of Marseilles began, with the King and Prime Minister seated together in the rear of the limousine. Georges, after shooting the arrival with a hand-held camera, ran down the street to get additional shots and then changed the magazine. Suddenly an assassin appeared from the crowd, jumped onto the running-board of the limousine and started to fire shots at the King, the Prime Minister, the crowd, and others in the official party. Just prior to all of this Georges had caught up with the procession and was in front of the official car filming when the action erupted. Grinding away furiously, he was able to capture the entire sequence, from before the appearance of the assassin to the firing of the many shots to the subsequent killing of the assassin by horse-mounted gendarmes wielding sabers. And finally, he filmed the king in deathly repose on the back seat of the automobile. (Barthou succumbed shortly thereafter at a hospital while being operated on for treatment of his wounds.) Subsequently the police decreed that the film footage could not be released, but by this time it was too late. Working with dispatch, the Mejats had already sent the film to Paris where prints were made and taken to Belgium, England, and Spain. All of this had been done before the police were able to act. And thus, as was to occur many times in the future, a seemingly ordinary event evolved into a filmed record of an extraordinary occurrence that would be viewed and discussed for many years to come. Whether by luck or pre-planning, Movietone was almost always on the scene and its film archives now constitute the most extensive photographic record of the events and people of the modern world.

THE END OF MOVIETONE

Movietone News was a profitable enterprise in the United States until around 1958-59, when the impact of television finally took its toll. At its zenith, newsreel activity was enormous, and the complement of personnel, resources, and facilities was similarly extensive. In addition to the bi-weekly production of newsreels, the issuance of specials, and the filming of short subjects and documentaries, Movietone had aggressively expanded its holdings (and also its archives) by acquiring pre-1919 material. Such acquisitions included the Wright Brothers' first flight, coverage of Teddy Roosevelt's Presidential campaign, Czar Nicholas IV of Russia with the Royal Family (1904), as well as his appearance at the front during WW I. This, combined with Fox-Movietone activities from its auspicious 1919 commencement, gave an unequalled overview of the 20th Century.

By 1960 Movietone had for all intents and purposes become a house promotion vehicle for the 20th Century-Fox Film Corp.; the staff, particularly cameramen, had been drastically reduced in number, and from the late 1950's on, very little news of a substantive nature appeared. On October 1, 1963, the last issue of Movietone News (United States) appeared in subscribing theaters and featured, rather dismally as well as tragically, an extended, interminable coverage of an endless cattle drive; an event that would have been interesting from the point of view of "natural" sound in 1929 but that in 1963 more than aptly indicated that the era of the newsreel was at a vainglorious end in the United States.

ACKNOWLEDGMENTS

A project of this magnitude could not possibly have come into being without a plethora of contributions by many individuals. My endless appreciation to the following. Tom Dunne, Senior Editor, and Barbara Walsh, Production Director of St. Martin's Press for making it all possible; to the staff of Movietonews, Inc.: Jack Muth, Vice President & General Manager, who was kind enough to share his wealth of experience, knowledge and reminiscences with me: Harold Potter, National Sales Manager, a constant source of amazement and amusement, who contributed greatly; and Evelyn Champion and Don Sills, Assistant Movietone Librarians. A very special note of thanks and an expression of appreciation as well as indebtedness to Nick Leary, Chief Librarian, Movietonews, Inc., whose overall contribution to the entire undertaking was enormous and can not be measured by mere words.

Thanks to Bill Fisher, Assistant Secretary, 20th Century-Fox, Inc. and Counsel to Movietonews, Inc.; Mike Prush, former Chief Librarian, who gave freely of his long Movietone tenure and who physically assisted in a very difficult situation; and to Bob Epstein, UCLA Film Archives, Bill Galloway, The National Film Archives, Canada, and the following friends and family whose understanding, assistance and encouragement were priceless: Michael Brooks, a friend in need as well as a friend in deed, who aided substantially in the research as well as myriad other areas, Gene Settler, Nancy Hamilton, Frank Driggs, Edward Rissien, Pete Welding, Edward Guy, my sister Gloria and family Beverly, Lee and Laurie.

An informational assist was provided by Raymond Fielding's "The American Newsreel—1911–1967." University of Oklahoma Press, 1972.

TO THE READER:

In researching the vast amount of material involved in putting this book together, close to one year was spent viewing several million feet of film on a small-screen movieola. For the most part, the original negatives have been used (most of which had not been run since the original date), and in many instances, early footage was luckily obtained just prior to its disintegration. I have made every effort to select the best frames available, though on some of the prints deterioration is, alas, noticeable.

In addition to literally millions of index cards and dope sheets there are roughly 5,000 continuity sheets, one for each issued newsreel and special, all of which were researched and analyzed in order to select and view footage. Thousands of frames were selected, developed, and considered. The final selections were made on the basis of interest, rarity, and relevance to the categories presented.

Although the overall coverage afforded by Movietone News was extensive, in-depth, and international, the filming of certain areas of human behavior was unavoidably not all-encompassing. This is quite evident in the field of sporting events, boxing in particular. Shots of the actual fights were few and far between, although contract signings, weigh-ins, and training camp activities were present in abundance. The primary reason for this was that the promoters of the events controlled filming rights of boxing matches, and the rights were generally sold to the highest bidder for extremely large sums. Further, there was a somewhat sketchy coverage of the arts; this omission may have been the result of a non-specific policy against covering, to any great degree, anything that would compete with feature films and theatrical entertainment.

A final technical note. There are instances in the book where an approximate date is employed in the caption text. This is because in a large number of cases the pertinent printed matter and records have been destroyed—sometimes by accident but sometimes out of ignorance or design. Also, wherever practical, we have endeavored to use captions exactly as they appeared in the body of the newsreel or in the printed continuity sheets; such usage is indicated by quotation marks.

Lawrence Cohn

TWENTIETH CENTURY PERSONALITIES

The filmed record of personalities captured by the cameras of Movietone News is seemingly endless. Appearances by virtually every person of note active in Twentieth-Century life—kings and queens, diplomats, sports figures, heads-of-state, motion picture and theater personages, literari, politicians, tyrants and dictators, presidents, inventors, explorers and military leaders—were preserved by Movietone's extended, on-the-spot coverage. In addition, interviews were recorded with such world figures as George Bernard Shaw, Arthur Conan Doyle, famous Italian poet and war hero Gabriel D'Annunzio and even dictator Benito Mussolini (in a specially prepared speech in English).

Many of these events were filmed specifically for the Movietone cameras and were in many instances the sole filmed interviews ever granted by the personalities. It is a tribute to the tenacity and vision of the directors and staff of Movietone that we do, indeed, have visual records of many of the most important, and often reclusive, figures of the Twentieth Century.

The twilight of an era. *Left:* A rare photograph from the Movietone archives of Tsar Nicholas II and his family at a family gathering in 1904. In 1918 they were executed by the Bolsheviks. *Below:* King George V of England at the funeral of his father, Edward VII, in 1910.

Far right: President Warren G. Harding, Washington, D.C., 1921.

Right: Woodrow Wilson, c. 1914.

Below: A rare picture of Teddy Roosevelt campaigning, c. 1900.

President Calvin Coolidge, one of the most taciturn chief executives in history, was a willing subject for the Movietone cameras. *Below,* he is entertained by a group of enthusiastic cowboys in 1925, and seriously considers shooting his wife for taking an unstaged photograph.

Financier J. P. Morgan testifies before the Pujo
Committee of Congress in 1912. He died the next
year. John D. Rockefeller *(right)* cracks an
uncharacteristic smile for the cameras in 1928,
but several years later seems unamused by Will
Rogers *(above)*.

Three statesmen, three political philosophies. *Above right:* Germany's aging von Hindenburg reviews troops as militarism reappears in Germany. *Below right:* Symbol of the new European democracies, President Masaryk of Czechoslovakia in 1934. *Below:* Lenin shortly after his accession to power in Russia.

Below: Leon Trotsky, the organizer of the Red Army, shown in a rare photo reviewing troops during the civil war of 1918–20. *Right:* Trotsky and his wife arrive in Mexico in 1937 after expulsion from Norway at Stalin's insistence. Three years later he was murdered at his Mexican villa.

Above: Generalissimo Chiang Kai-shek, 1920's.
Right: "Gandhi stirs civil disorder in India; rioting spreads. With the Japanese poised on the border, the little agitator leads a revolt, rejecting British guarantee of independence for India after the war." 1942.

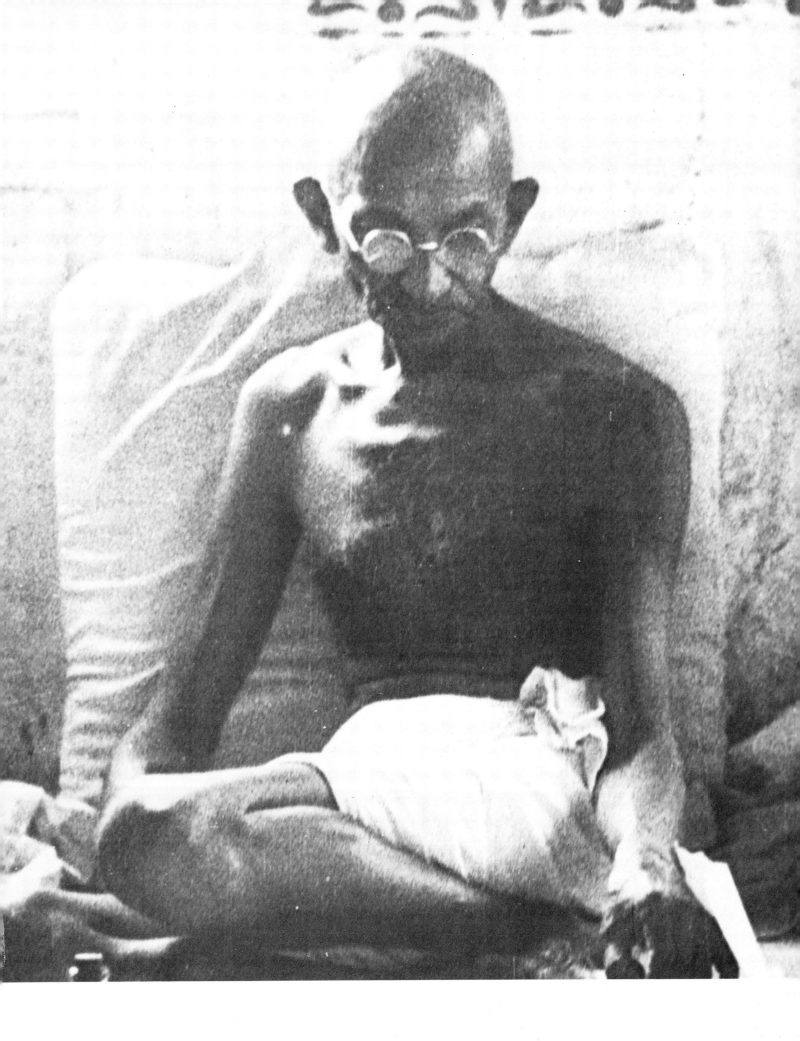

A crisis that shook the throne of England. *Above left:* King Edward VIII in 1936, shortly before his abdication. *Above right:* The former King after his marriage to Mrs. Simpson. *Below:* Princess Margaret, 10-year-old Elizabeth and the Duke of York, soon to be King George VI.

Above: Mary, Queen Mother of England, in 1945. *Below:* Three generations of the Royal Family attend the wedding of Princess Elizabeth to Prince Philip of Greece. 1947.

Movietone cameras followed the Royal Family with great interest. *Below:* The Duke of Windsor (Edward VIII) and Wallis Warfield Simpson on their wedding day. 1937. *Above right:* Queen Elizabeth visits a Welsh coal mine. 1958. *Below right:* "Princess Elizabeth, sixteen years old, inspects the Grenadier Guards." 1942. One of the guards could not resist a second look at the heir to the throne.

Perhaps the greatest—and certainly one of the most controversial—
dancers of her time, Isadora Duncan is here caught in her most creative
period, the 1920's.

Above: W. C. Fields on the golf course. 1928.

Left: Rudolph Valentino, 1920's.

"The famous 'It' girl of the silent screen, Clara Bow,
is happy in her new 'It' Cafe." 1937.

The most popular actor of his time, Tom Mix, is honored by a parade in
Fresno and by Fox executives, 1926.

Above: Mix tries his hand at pitching. *Below:* His film is a box-office smash in the Australian outback.

Will Rogers, Beverly Hills, Ca. c. 1926. The great American humorist loved machinery, particularly fire engines. Here he is appointed honorary fire chief of Beverly Hills.

Harry Houdini, the acclaimed escape artist and magician who performed feats never attempted before or since. Note newsreel cameraman on ledge, *above,* as Houdini succeeds once again.

WANTED

JOHN HERBERT DILLINGER

On June 23, 1934, HOMER S. CUMMINGS, Attorney General of the United States, under the authority vested in him by an Act of Congress approved June 6, 1934, offered a reward of

$10,000.00

for the capture of John Herbert Dillinger or a reward of

$5,000.00

for information leading to the arrest of John Herbert Dillinger.

John Herbert Dillinger, Public Enemy Number One and one of the most successful criminals of his time, was finally brought down in 1934. Movie audiences were treated to the results of a life of crime *(below)*.

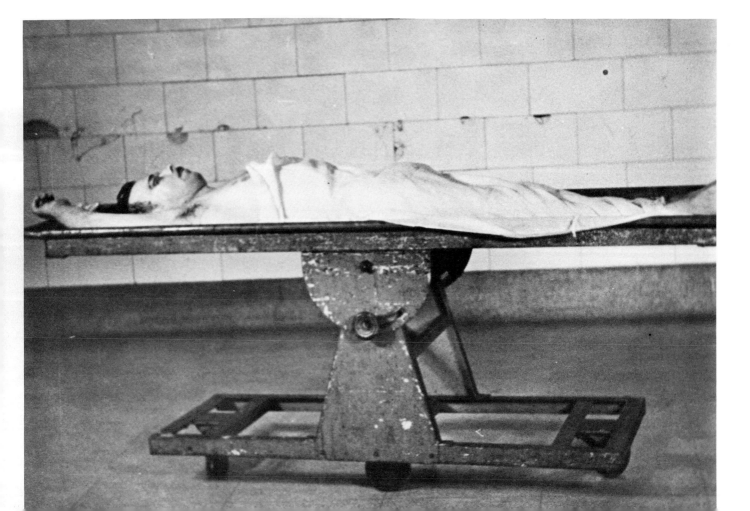

Above: "Charlie Chaplin and Pauline (sic) Goddard
return from a trip to the Orient and put on an act
for Movietone's reporter." 1936. *Right:* "Entertainer
George M. Cohan welcomed home, Providence, R. I."
1934. *Above, far right:* Eddie Cantor and Samuel
Goldwyn, 1930. *Below, far right:* Mayor Jimmy Walker
of New York City, George Jessel and Eddie Cantor,
1927.

Evangelist Aimee Semple McPherson in 1929. A controversial preacher,
she built the huge Angelus Temple in Los Angeles. When she died,
a live telephone was installed in her coffin . . . just in case.

Below: "Bishop Grace baptizes his colored flock by immersion and all God's chillun need water wings." Virginia, 1936. *Left:* Evangelist Billy Graham, Wimbledon Stadium, England.

Below: "Henry Ford and Herbert Hoover visit shrine of Abraham Lincoln and pay homage at the building where he practiced law." 1937.
Above right: Henry Ford and Thomas Alva Edison, Chautauqua, New York, 1929. *Below right:* "Clarence Darrow, renowned Chicago lawyer, attacks NRA policies, saying monopoly is aided." 1934.

Above: General Douglas MacArthur, Philippines, c. 1936.
Above right: "Jack Benny pulls his own scrap blitz and brings his famous
Maxwell to the junk pile." 1942. *Below right:* "Movie star Hedy Lamarr,
on her tour for sale of War Bonds, draws a great crowd in Newark." 1942.

Above: Boxer Jack Johnson leads a jazz band at his nightclub in New York 1930. *Below:* Ed Sullivan, 1936.

Two of America's funniest men. *Above:* Joe E. Brown
in 1936. *Below:* The great Fred Allen, c. 1946.

Above: "Gene Autry has Oklahoma town named for him. The town of Berwyn changes its name in tribute to famous movie star of western pictures." 1941. *Below:* "Troops of Santa Ana, California Air Base are entertained by Bing Crosby and Bob Hope, the movie comedians putting on a great show." 1944.

Above: George Burns, Jack Benny, Bob Hope, Joe DiMaggio and Groucho Marx. "Stars assist charity and headline the Damon Runyon Cancer Fund ball game." 1953. *Below:* Comedians Bud Abbott and Lou Costello with Fiorello La Guardia, Mayor of New York City, 1943.

Above left: Mussolini attends a harvest festival in 1937. With him is his mistress, Clara Petacci, who was executed with him in 1945. *Below left:* "Tito of Yugoslavia filmed in hide-out with partisans." 1944.
Above: Churchill is guest of honor at NATO review, 1957.

Above left: Eleanor and Franklin Delano Roosevelt, The White House, Washington, D.C., 1936. *Below left:* Eleanor Roosevelt, on one of her countless goodwill trips, in this instance for the Red Cross. 1955. *Below:* "President Roosevelt and General Douglas MacArthur during conference with Pacific War Leaders in Hawaii," 1944. A few months after this was shot, Roosevelt was dead.

Below: "President Roosevelt and running mate Harry Truman confer. Democratic Presidential and Vice Presidential candidates discuss plans in Washington for the 1944 campaign." *Above right:* "Ex-President Harry Truman has duet with head of Musicians' Union. Guest of honor at a Milwaukee Convention, the former President joins James Petrillo to entertain delegates." 1954. *Below right:* "Historic meeting of President Truman and General MacArthur on Wake Island. After their important talk on the Korean War and peace, Truman decorates MacArthur and then each returns to his job in the U.S. and Tokyo." 1950.

ALABAMA
WE LIKE
IKE
TEXAS
FOR
ET'S WIN
IKE IN,
LET'S WIN
EEP IKE IN
WE LIK
IKE

Above: President Eisenhower welcomes England's Queen Mother. 1956.
Below: Secretary of State John Foster Dulles and President Dwight Eisenhower, 1954.

Above: Senator John Kennedy's wedding in 1953. Bobby Kennedy is at the left. Shortly after his election in 1960, Kennedy exudes confidence in a meeting with outgoing President Eisenhower *(above right)*. *Below right:* Lyndon B. Johnson addresses Congress.

Above: Governor of Louisiana Huey P. Long, c. 1934.
Above right: Senator Richard M. Nixon studies evidence in the Whittaker Chambers—Alger Hiss spy trial. 1949. *Below right:* "Columnist loses bet and eats his hat. Before the Capitol, Drew Pearson pays off on an election wager." 1948.

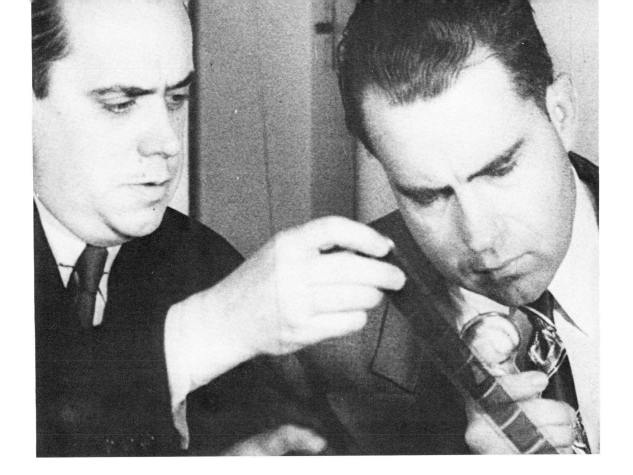

Above: "Hearty, hilarious handshakings mark Nikita–Mao meeting. The fabulous meeting in Peiping of the two tyrants of Communism, Nikita Khrushchev and Mao Tse-tung." 1958. *Above right:* "Soviet leaders eat humble pie to court Tito. At Belgrade, Yugoslavia's Chief plays host to Russian strong-men Khrushchev and Bulganin." 1955. *Below right:* "Soviet Prime Minister Nikita Khrushchev visits Hollywood and the set of 'Can Can,' meeting the stars of the forthcoming spectacle, Shirley MacLaine, Frank Sinatra, Maurice Chevalier and Louis Jourdan." 1959.

Above: "Communism's traditional fete day is the occasion for Premier Castro to stage a monster rally in Havana." 1960. Below: "The Congo's deposed Premier Lumumba, after capture by troops of Col. Mobutu, is jeered as a traitor as he is whisked to jail." 1960. Above right: "General Moshe Dayan with victorious Israeli troops as they capture thousands of Egyptians and take complete control of the Gaza Strip." 1956. Below right: Pope Pius XII, Vatican City, 1954.

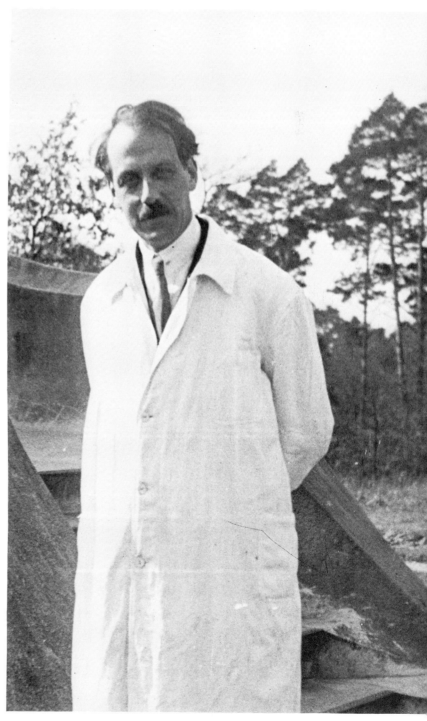

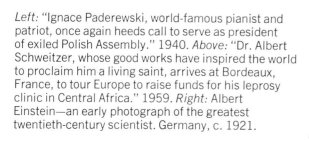

Left: "Ignace Paderewski, world-famous pianist and patriot, once again heeds call to serve as president of exiled Polish Assembly." 1940. *Above:* "Dr. Albert Schweitzer, whose good works have inspired the world to proclaim him a living saint, arrives at Bordeaux, France, to tour Europe to raise funds for his leprosy clinic in Central Africa." 1959. *Right:* Albert Einstein—an early photograph of the greatest twentieth-century scientist. Germany, c. 1921.

Above: George Bernard Shaw, c. 1928.

Below: William Somerset Maugham and friend, c. 1960.

Above: "St. Lawrence University honors Madame Curie, the 'mother of radium,' a well-deserved tribute to the greatest of all women scientists." 1929. *Below:* "Lord Baden-Powell, founder of Boy Scouts, celebrates 80th birthday in India attending Jamboree at Delhi." 1937.

Below: Ernest Hemingway in Africa shortly after surviving an airplane crash. 1954. *Right:* "Ernie Pyle, famous war correspondent, killed in Ryukyus. Idol of G.I. Joe, popular newspaperman covered the war in Africa, Europe and the Pacific. Narrowly missing death at Anzio beachhead, Pyle was shot by a Jap (sic) machine gunner." 1945.
Below right: Marian Anderson sings in front of the Lincoln Memorial, Washington, D.C. 1939.

Above: Rudyard Kipling, c. 1935. *Below:* "At Vallauris, on the French Riviera, famed Spanish modernist Pablo Picasso sees an exhibition of his works and a bullfight staged to mark his 80th birthday." 1961.

Above: Carl Sandburg and his brother-in-law, photographer Edward Steichen, c. 1960. *Below:* "Artist Norman Rockwell paints actress Jennifer Jones, featured in the 20th Century-Fox picture, 'Song of Bernadette.'" 1943.

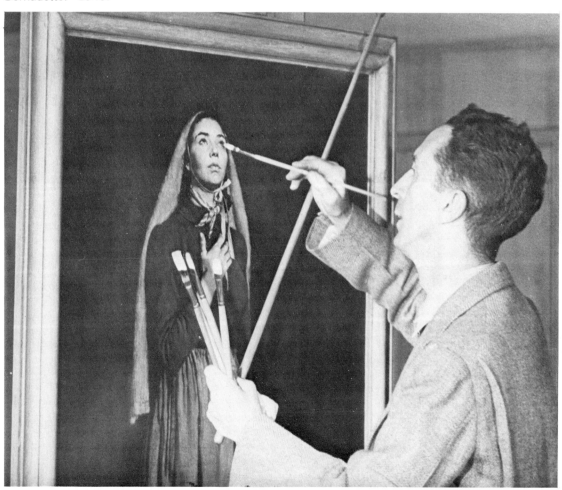

Academy Awards, Hollywood, 1963.
Sammy Davis, Jr., Barbra Streisand,
Mr. and Mrs. Steve McQueen, Sandra
Dee and Bobby Darin, Julie Andrews.

One of the greatest stars of all time, Marilyn Monroe. *Above left:*
With Joe DiMaggio shortly after their marriage. *Below left:*
Marilyn Monroe and Jane Russell immortalized in cement. 1953. *Below:*
Lauren Bacall and a wistful Marilyn.

Elvis Presley with guitarist Scotty Moore, as RCA Victor Mascot listens
to his master's voice.

FASHIONS

In providing coverage of fashions the Movietone newsreel primarily functioned as a women's page and rarely touched upon the subject of men's fashions. Concerning itself with trends and *style,* as well as the humorous and offbeat, its subjects were ingenious and far-reaching. Present from the inception of the Fox newsreel, the fashion coverage was an eagerly anticipated and well-received segment of each program and presented a worldwide overview of fashion and the changing tastes in dress along with some salient and frequently pithy commentary.

Vyvyan Donner, Fashion Editor, and Louise Vance and Helen Claire, the fashion commentators, were three of the individuals who shaped and structured Movietone's fashion coverage; Jack Painter and Carl Larsen did much of the filming. Their combined efforts resulted in one of the most interesting and popular portions of the Movietone saga.

One of Movietone's first fashion shows in 1919 (below and on the following three pages) featured intricate needlework and long, flowing garments. The show began with a thoroughly impractical and very patriotic ballgown.

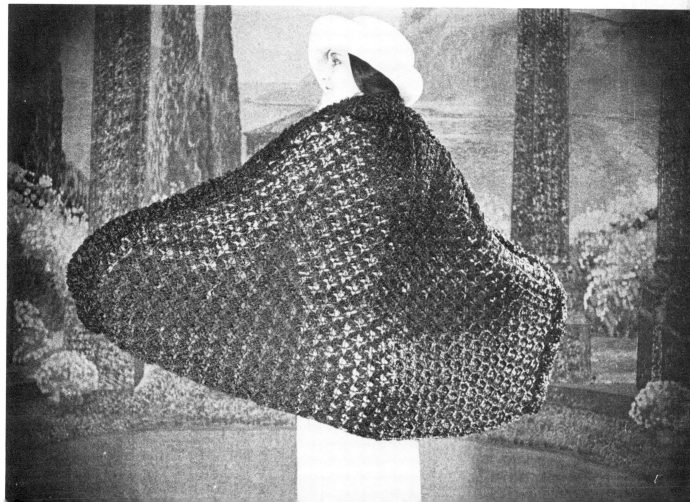

San Francisco styles, c. 1922.

"Elegance and simplicity are the
hallmarks of fashion today." 1919.

Feathers and furs, c. 1921.

The heart-throb of America's women, Rudolph Valentino, inspired a brief flurry of "sheik" fashions, c. 1925.

Hems began to rise as the twenties progressed, though the accent was still on elaborate designs and flowing, expensive fabrics. Here, and on the following two pages, are the latest designs of 1925.

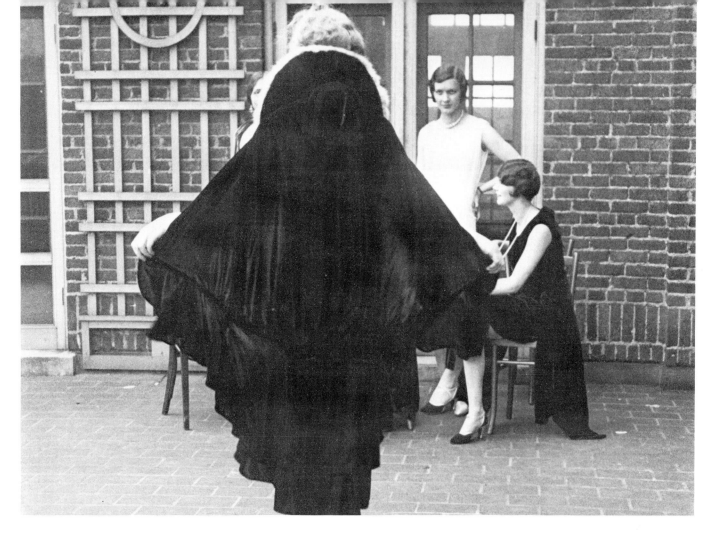

High fashion in the later 1920's. The hat at right is suggested in Movietone's 1926 fashion show "for important occasions."

The Paris fashions of 1924 left something to be desired, particularly those below. On the opposite page, an idea whose time never came: fur coats (rabbit) for beachwear.

"Broadway dancers model the latest in beachwear." 1929.

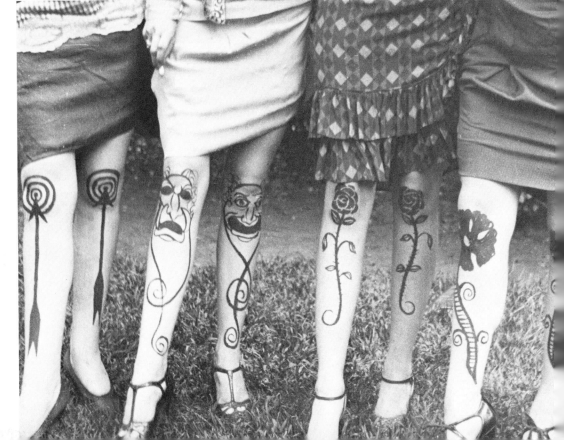

Leg-painting was a recurrent fad. *Above left*, 1924. *Below left*, c. 1935. *Right*, 1950. *Below*, some handsome shoes, the ones on the right in the art-deco style, c. 1926.

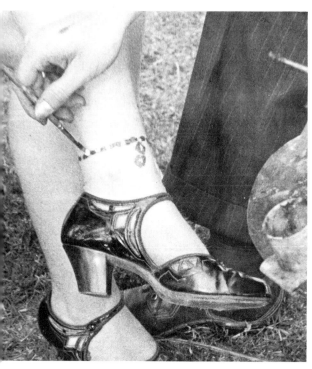

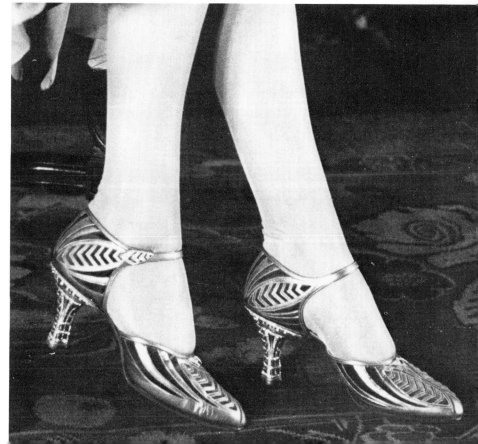

Fashions of the 1920's and early '30's. The beautiful picture hat (or is it just the beautiful girl?), c. 1929.

FRAULEINS DISPLAY NEWEST PRETTIES

Berlin mannequins let you
have an intimate view of
what the German girls
wear in their sleep

Fox Movietone News

The news from Germany, 1920. Why must three girls share one bed? And who is the man with the moustache? The silent captions did not explain.

Beachwear. *Left,* c. 1900, *right,* 1925.

Lavish or expensive coats were a staple of Movietone's fashion shows. *Below left*, a 1921 snakeskin coat. The 1927 mink was of a more than ample design.

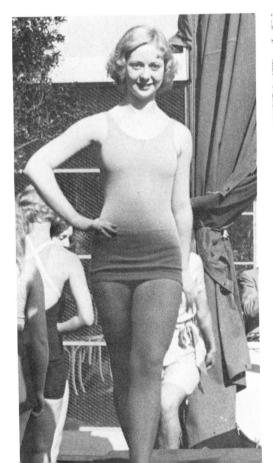

"Meet Broadway's prize show girl. Violet Carson is picked as prettiest and shapeliest of all the chorines on the Gay White Way."
1930.

"Hats for the World's Fair!
Forthcoming show inspires striking,
and some startling, ideas for the
head—but not for the theatre." 1938.

Some sights for sore eyes. Movietone cameras recorded the latest in ocular fashions. *Left:* One of the truly hideous fashion ideas of the twentieth century, Harlequin glasses, 1958, and their logical extreme —Harlequin sunglasses, 1961. *Below:* A dignified monocle, c. 1924.

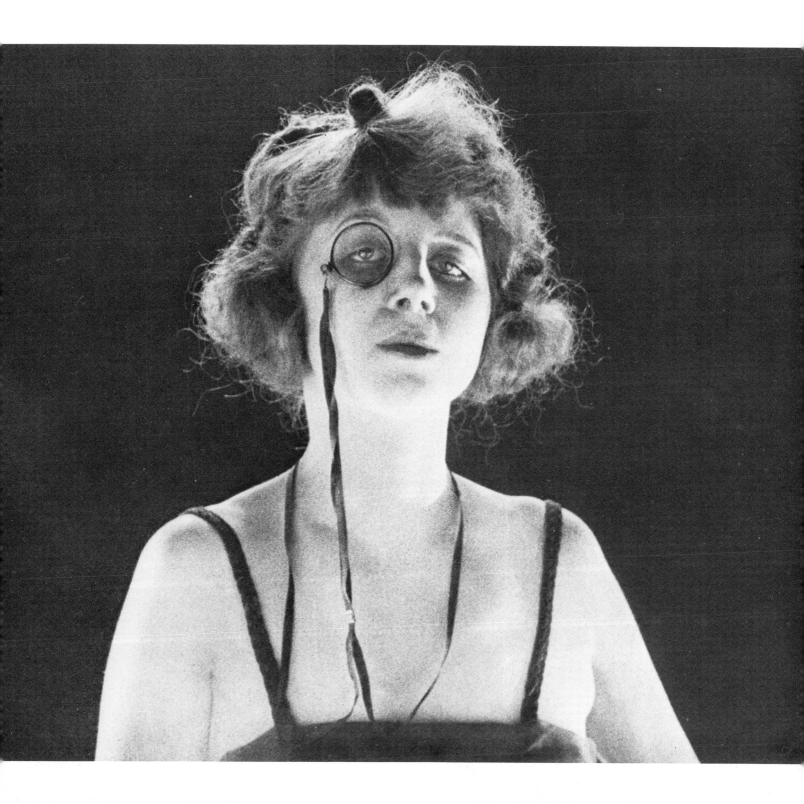

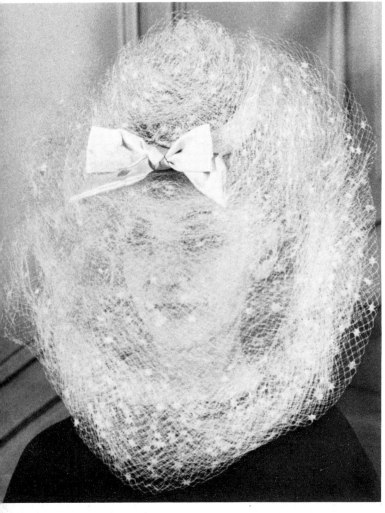

Paris designers show their wares in the early 1950's.
The hat and accessories *(below right)* are entirely
made out of plastic.

WAR IN THE TWENTIETH CENTURY

From its inception, Movietone's reportage of war and local conflict was one of the most recurrent of all human activities covered by its cameras. The timely and informative nature of this part of the firm's operation, and its success as well, was due in no small measure to men such as Laurence Stallings, Truman Talley, Lowell Thomas, Edmund Reek, Gerald Sanger, Sir Malcolm Campbell, Sir Gordon Craig, Russell Muth, Jack Haney, Louis Tetunic, Jack Muth, Burt Reinhardt, Ben Loweree, Joe King, Ben Miggins, and many others.

The coverage of war and conflict throughout the years was all-embracing and frequently monumental in achievement. In many cases obtaining footage at genuine peril to life, Movietone cameramen such as Bonney Powell, Eric Mayell, in the Far East and others throughout the world were ever-present through the years at the front lines of more conflicts than memory cares to recollect. They were there during the Sino-Japanese conflict in Manchuria, in Barcelona during the Spanish Civil War as destruction rained from bombers overhead, in Ethiopia when Mussolini's well-equipped legions attacked the tribal armies of Emperor Haile Selassie, in Vienna to view Hitler's triumphant entrance, at the Panay incident where, in 1937, a United States Navy ship was sunk by the Japanese, in the South Pacific as well as throughout Europe during WW II, at France's Maginot Line on the eve of the Second World War and the impending German invasion, and in Korea, French Indo-China and Vietnam. The list is endless and the visual record enduring and breathtaking.

Newsreel viewers followed the development of World War I from its very beginning. *Right:* General John Pershing congratulating a young Douglas MacArthur, 1917.

EXTRA!

Oakland Tribune

WAR!

GERMANS LAUNCH FRENCH ATTACK

$60,000 Damage in Gigantic BALLOT AWAITED | TWO OKLAHOMA CONVICTS SHOOT GUARD AND ESCAPE | APPEAL TO GAIN RACKET MURDER EXTRADITION OF DEFENDANTS TO | Powerful Forces

L'ARMISTICE EST SIGNE

LA GUERRE EST GAGNEE

VIVE LA FRANCE! VIVENT LES ALLIES!

EXTRA!

Oakland Tribune

3 CENTS

THREE CENTS

ARMISTICE!
GUNS FALL SILENT!
FIGHTING CEASES AT 11 A. M.

ARMISTICE TERMS

World Overjoyed As
Good News Is Heard

WAR ENDED

...ember 11—The World War
ended this morning at 6 o'clock,

Germany in the 1920's was torn by dissent. While von Hindenburg represented the old militaristic values of Prussia (note single Nazi salute), others rallied in anti-war demonstrations.

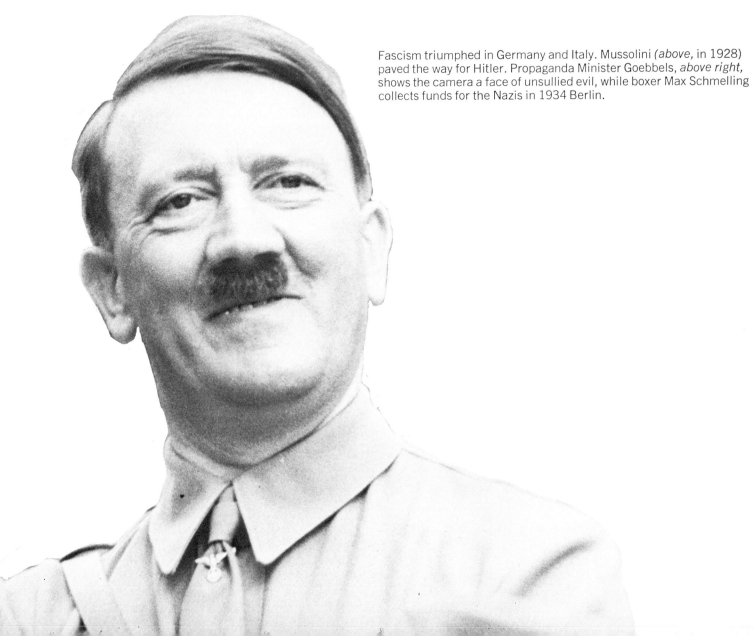

Fascism triumphed in Germany and Italy. Mussolini (above, in 1928) paved the way for Hitler. Propaganda Minister Goebbels, above right, shows the camera a face of unsullied evil, while boxer Max Schmelling collects funds for the Nazis in 1934 Berlin.

Hitler's Nuremberg rallies impressed and frightened the world. *Left: Der Führer* reviews 450,000 brownshirts in 1935. *Below:* S.S. troops march in review.

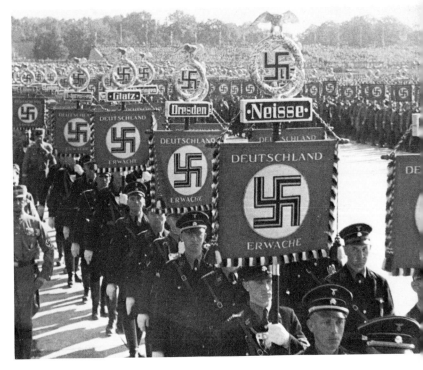

Movietone sent film crews to cover both sides of the Spanish Civil War. *Below:* "Victorious rebel forces capture Toledo and continue to push on to Madrid." 1936. *Right:* "Dramatic films, just received from cameramen risking their lives within the beleaguered capital of Madrid, depicts a soldier being shot and killed!" 1936.

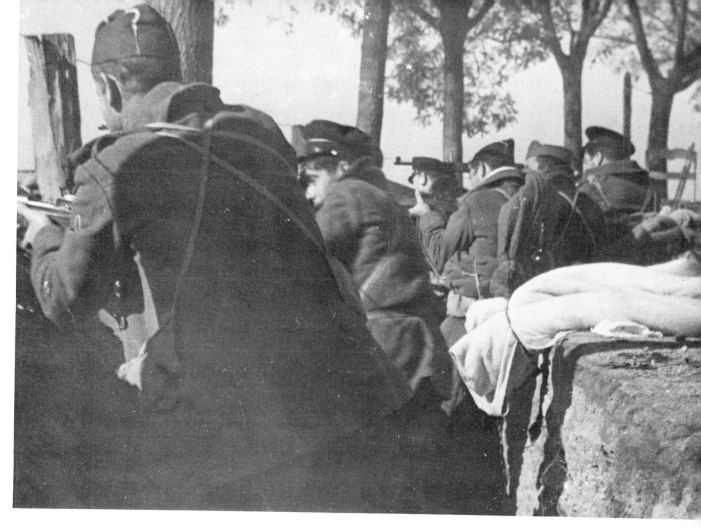

Left: As the Civil War progressed in Spain, city after city was shelled and levelled. *Below:* "Marshall Pétain meets Gen. Franco in Montpellier, France. Spanish Chief confers with Pétain after visit to Mussolini in Italy." 1941.

"England ready for action in
Ethiopian crisis. British air
garrison on outskirts of Cairo
keeps patrol over the land of the
Nile." 1935.

"Addis Ababa prepares for war as Mussolini defies the League of
Nations. Tribal chieftains arrive at capital eager to place
themselves at the service of Emperor Haile Selassie. Meanwhile,
Ethiopia's new army completes training and well-drilled regiments
in bare feet march to the front." 1935.

"Latest pictures from the China War Front. Refugees stream from
Shanghai, city of death." 1937.

Above: "Mongolia. Soviet-Japanese mystery war. Though countries are formally at peace, reporters see captured prisoners." 1939. *Below:* British troops help refugees escape as Shanghai is shelled.

"Japanese Army begins encircling movement around Shanghai. Nippon's troops attack in a new strategy to cut off defending Chinese forces in the city. Movietone cameraman advances with invaders to film capture of Tangkwantun, north of Shanghai." 1937. *Above right:* Japanese troops celebrate capture of Shanghai. *Below right:* "Nippon parades its imposing mechanized army in review before Emperor Hirohito." 1934.

Above: "Premier Mussolini passes entire military might before Hitler. Grand finale in Rome is spectacular march before assembled dignitaries." 1938. *Left:* Chamberlain and Mussolini. Rome, 1938.

Above: Following the murder of Chancellor Dollfuss by Austrian Nazis, Vienna is placed under military control. 1934. *Below:* "Germany annexes Austrian Republic. Europe in turmoil. Hitler seen in triumphant entry, whole populace at his feet." 1938.

On the Maginot Line before the German *blitzkrieg:* "Movietone Producer Truman Talley, with European Movietone officials, studies the war front first hand, first civilian observation party ever permitted to visit. Investigating the war picture problem, the newsreel executive inspects extensive French fortifications." 1940.

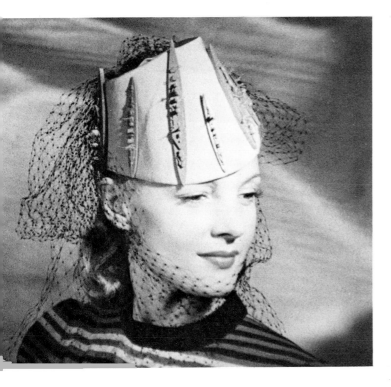

Above: "War scare influences Paris hats. With Europe on edge in tense situations, the Parisian milliners get startling ideas for headwear. Chapeaux are decorated with airplanes, tanks and battleships or are designed like gas masks." 1939. *Left:* "Londoners still dancing. The slogan is 'Carry your gas mask,' so dance becomes a masked ball, but it's fun for brave English." 1941.

Above left: President Franklin D. Roosevelt reviews the fleet, c. 1935. Below left: "The Nazi pocket battleship Graf Spee, defeated in a battle off Montevideo, Uruguay, just prior to being deliberately scuttled and sunk." 1939. Above right: "General MacArthur creates an army. Former U.S. Chief of Staff explains military force he is forming to defend Philippines' national integrity." 1936. Below right: "Selective Service drawing is held in Washington. A dramatic event in history of the United States. Secretary of War Stimson, blindfolded, draws from the same fishbowl used in the first World War draft. President Roosevelt then announces the selection, number 158." 1940.

Above: The Battle of Britain. "Devastation as a result of Nazi air attacks in London." 1940. *Right:* "Churchill returns to U.S. for parlays. Back in Washington, D.C., he goes to church with President Roosevelt." 1942.

Movietone cameraman Al Brick *(above left)* caught on film the only motion pictures of the Japanese attack on Pearl Harbor. The scenes he recorded showed such destruction that they were seized by the government and shown to the public only after they had been censored.

Above: "On the Eastern Front. In Poland, Hitler mingles with troops and fraternizes with his men." 1939. *Below:* Captured film shows a German U-Boat attacking a convoy in 1943.

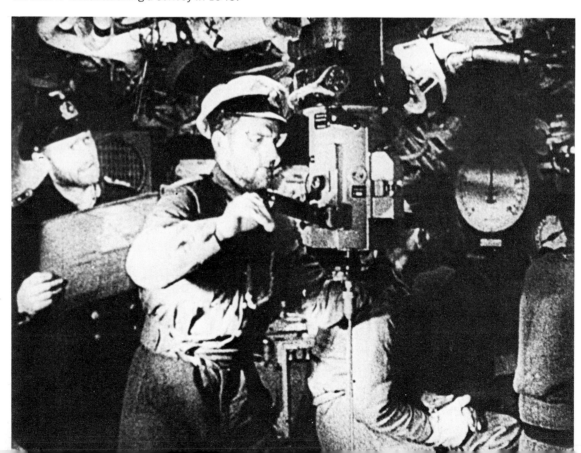

Industrial production surged as America went to war. "Women in war.
In a contest held at Sausalito, Calif., shipyard workers elect their
own "Miss Victory" as a typical woman in war." 1943.

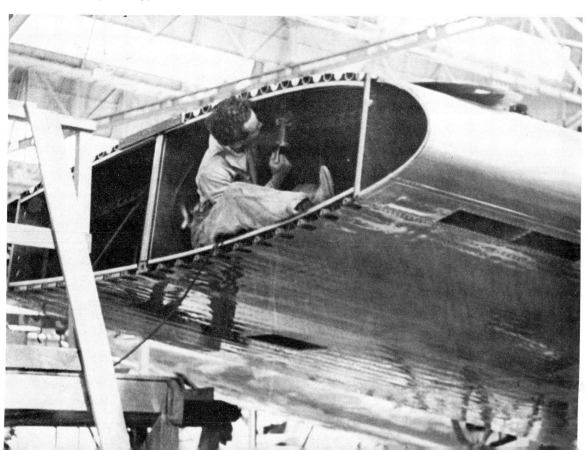

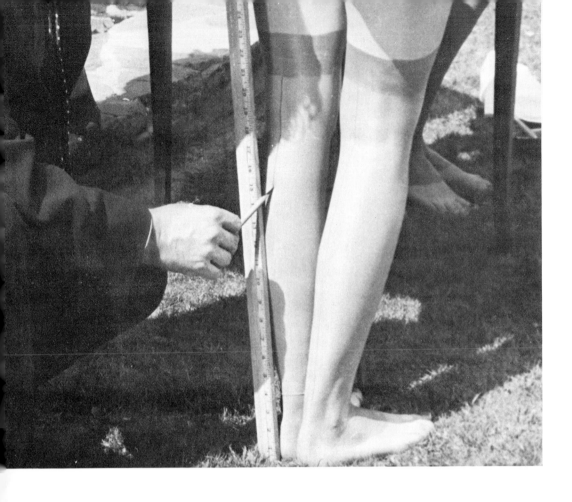

The Home Front. "Worried about silk embargo, girls? Take a tip from Hollywood. Movie starlets show they can't be stopped. They have famous make-up artists, the Westmores, paint stockings on their legs." 1941.

"Der Führer's Face, a picturization of a popular song that will make A. Schickelgruber's face redder than ever, sung by Spike Jones and the City Slickers." 1942. "Join the drive to smash the Axis and help win the war. The entire nation must cooperate in vital job of collecting old metal." 1942.

Movietone cameras recorded a carrier crash landing in the 1943 Pacific
campaign. The pilot was uninjured.

Left: "Following his overthrow, Italian dictator Mussolini was put in prison, then later rescued by German paratroopers." A rare and dramatic captured film. 1943. *Above:* "The gruesome end of Benito Mussolini, executed by Italian patriots. Duce's body is put on display in Milan, reviled by people, and then hung by the heels." 1945.

Above far left: "The bombing of Cassino Abbey. Pictures depict complete devastation of ancient monastery, fortified by the Nazis. High explosives smash the building as the enemy takes refuge in deep underground tunnels." 1944. *Above left:* American soldiers in Germany trade their helmets for more formal wear. 1945. *Below far left:* Shortly after D-Day, G.I.'s pose for the camera with captured trophies. *Below left:* Audie Murphy, the most decorated American war hero. France, 1945. *Right:* "Blood and Guts." General George S. Patton, 1944.

Above: "Dramatic film, in a sensational episode of the war, shows military units shooting at snipers." Paris, 1944. *Right:* "Liberation of Paris. Day of rejoicing in the lives of all free men. Paris goes delirious with joy." 1944. *Right above and below:* Architects of victory. DeGaulle at liberation of Paris. FDR and Churchill, 1943.

Above: "Women traitors. Female collaborationists are punished by local French patriots after the Nazis have been chased out. The women are shorn bald and turned out of town." *Left:* "In a wild rage, a crowd of Frenchmen vents its fury on a German." *Right:* "Last days of the war in Germany, liberated French captives return to their homes." 1945.

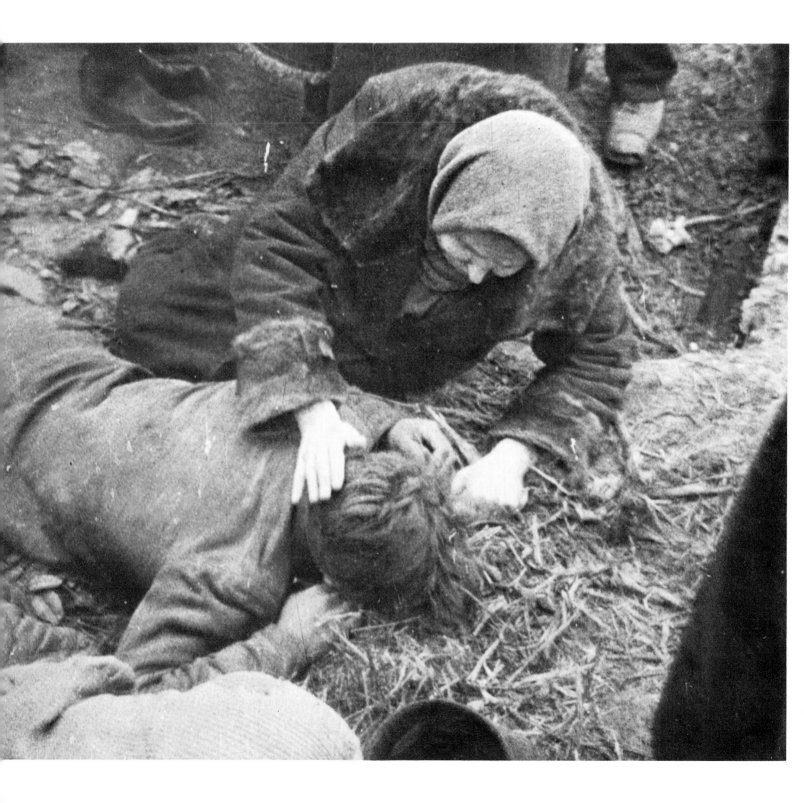

The face of war. *Above:* French children learn of their parents'
death. 1945. *Right:* A weary soldier following the capture of
Cherbourg in 1944.

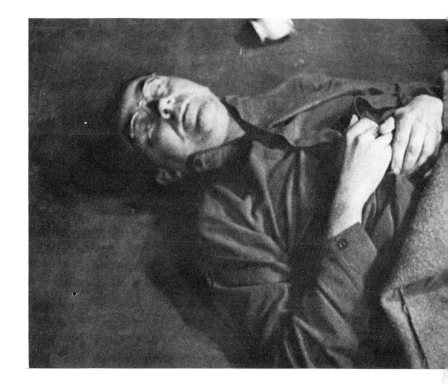

Left: Field Marshal Keitel
surrenders to allied troops in
1945. The next year he was
convicted of war crimes at Nuremberg
and hanged. *Right:* "Hangman's end.
Heinrich Himmler, the Nazi Gestapo
chief, kills himself by taking
poison after being apprehended by
British troops." 1945. *Below:* Nazi
Reichmarshal Hermann Goering
surrenders. 1945.

Hiroshima, 1945.

Left: "Film of Tokyo Rose who 'entertained' G.I.s in Pacific. Pictures just released show the Japanese-American girl reenacting the way she broadcast to U.S. troops at the front. Graduate from an American college, she wants to return to the U.S. where she may face treason charges." 1948. *Below left:* "47-year-old Mildred Gillars, born in Maine, is brought to Washington. She broadcast for Nazi Germany during World War II and was known to G.I.'s as Axis Sally. Now she is held without bail, awaiting trial on treason charges." 1948. *Below:* The infamous Ilsa Koch, "The Beast of Buchenwald," on trial for war crimes. 1947. *Right:* "Tojo takes stand in war crimes trial at Tokyo. Prime Minister when Japan launched the war in the Pacific and attacked Pearl Harbor, Tojo takes full responsibility." 1948. *Below right:* "Marshal Pétain on trial. Treason is the charge against ex-chief of Vichy government that collaborated with Nazi Germany. The aged hero of Verdun claims he secretly assisted Allies against the Nazis." 1945.

"Shanghai witnesses public execution of Chinese Reds. Scenes of stark drama and grim realism are photographed in the city imperiled by the advancing Communist armies. Reds, who were arrested and condemned for plotting a terrorist uprising, are taken to the street and shot to death as 100,000 swarm to see Chinese justice done." 1949. *Opposite:* Mao Tse-tung, c. 1939.

Right: "South Korean volunteers are outfitted with G.I. equipment and supplies and will be integrated in U.S. units." *Below:* "As Red offensives threaten vital city of Taegu, British troops arrive at Pusan." 1950. *Left:* Scenes from the battle of "Pork Chop Hill."

The human cost of war. "Korea.
Latest films of devastated Seoul
show why we must remain strong."
1951.

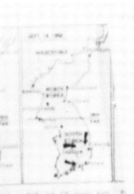

DAILY ⊕ NEWS

NEW YORK'S PICTURE NEWSPAPER

★★★ FINAL

4¢

KOREAN TRUCE SIGNED!

Strife Are Ov

(Stories on pages 2, 3, 4 and 15. Pictures in centerfold.)

Left: "French battle Indo-China Reds. Colonial troops clear out a section southeast of Saigon harassed by force of Communist-led Viet Minh guerrillas." 1950. The Movietone commentator goes on to note that the operation on the lower right is searching for "the last few Reds in Indochina." *Below:* "Red Mystery Man finally filmed. First pictures of Indo-China's Communist boss Ho Chi-Minh." 1954.

Left and below left: "Over 100 dead as settlers and Arabs clash with troops. Violence erupts between the colonists and Moslems calling for troops to separate and disperse them." 1960. *Below right:* "Revolt in Algiers collapses as France rallies to back DeGaulle." 1961.

After almost half a century of recording on film the human proclivity for self-destruction, the Congolese strife in 1963 was the last war Movietone covered. *Left:* Movietone cameramen risked their lives to film rioting in the Congo, 1963. *Below:* "While filming clashes in Katanga, a startling drama is recorded. A tragedy caused when a driver, ordered to halt, speeded up and drew a deadly fire killing his wife and a friend and being badly wounded himself."

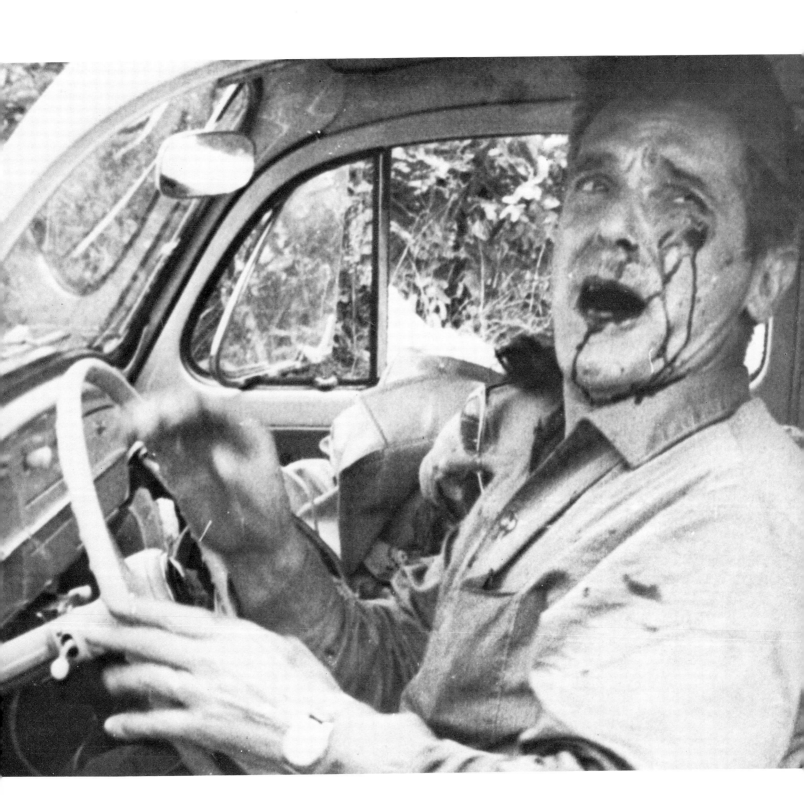

THE HUMAN SIDE

By its very definition, coverage of the area of human interest was varied and extraordinarily far-reaching. It included fads and follies, the unusual, music, entertainment, tragedy and myriad other aspects of daily life. A tightrope walker between two skyscrapers in downtown Chicago, flagpole sitters during the 1920's, Charleston contests, marathon dancers, a jug-band in Kentucky and a Broadway beauty contest featuring show girls were just a few of life's vignettes that were covered. Two of the better-known commentators were Ed Sullivan and Jimmie Fidler.

Lew Lehr, employer of the tag-line "monkees is the cwaziest people," was the individual who was primarily responsible for the offbeat and humorous "news-ettes" sequences; his was the comic-relief portion of Movietone's newsreels. Originally a Fox short-subjects editor, his acting abilities and talent for comedy were well employed as both commentator and participant as he sought out the oddities of life. Forever using a middle name relating to the subject matter (Lew "Cold Feet" Lehr when reporting on bathers who were referred to as "human polar bears"; Lew "Also Ran" Lehr when at the race track; Lew "Chump for Chimps" when dealing with the species), he was probably second only to Lowell Thomas in popularity and identification with the entire Movietone News operation.

"Tennessee he-man survives shave with a wood cleaver." *Right:* a 1937 beauty aid—the hot-water-bottle-wrinkle-removing-relaxing face mask. For some reason, this never caught on.

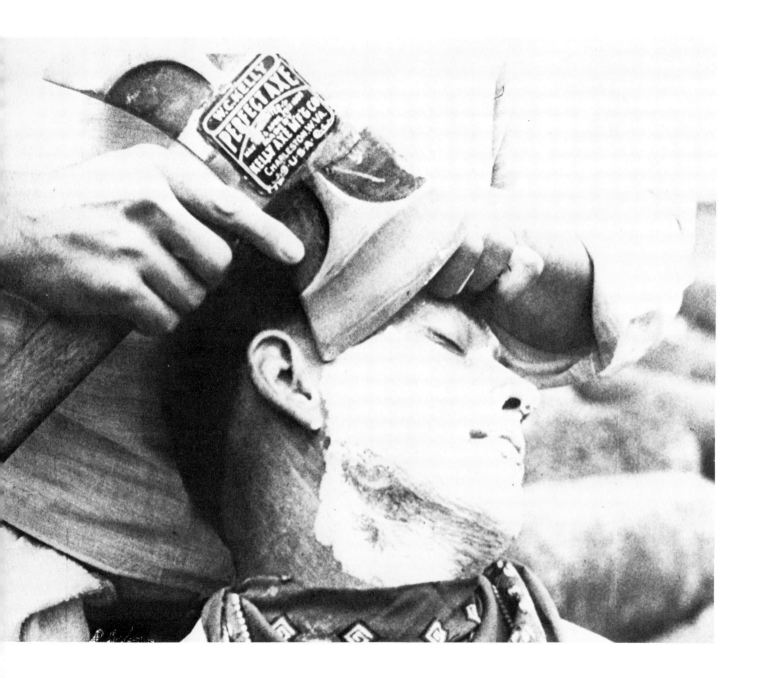

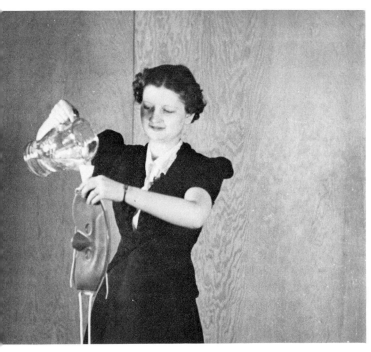
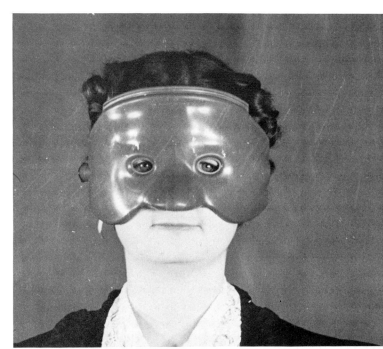

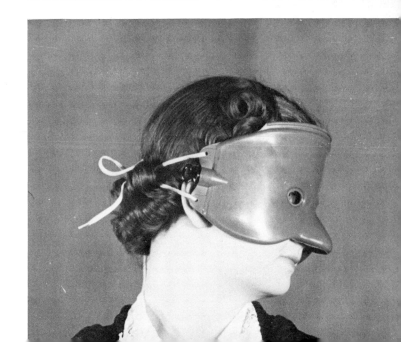

Right: A fad of the late twenties (one of many), marathon balancing many stories above ground. In this picture, a brother and sister team stood above Fifth Avenue in New York for close to twenty-four hours. *Below:* Jim Terry does his stuff with nothing between him and the Chicago pavement 39 stories below." 1929.

Famed flag-pole sitter Shipwreck
Kelly, c. 1923.

"Old swimmin' hole New York style. Crowd of 1,000,000 big city men, women and children seek relief from the heat in surf at Coney Island." 1932. *Left:* A look back. The reunion of the last survivors of the Battle of Shiloh, 1921.

Particularly after the advent of sound, Movietone regularly featured a musical segment. *Below:* A gathering of New England country fiddlers, Providence, R.I., c. 1921. *Right:* A folk music festival, Asheville, N.C., 1930.

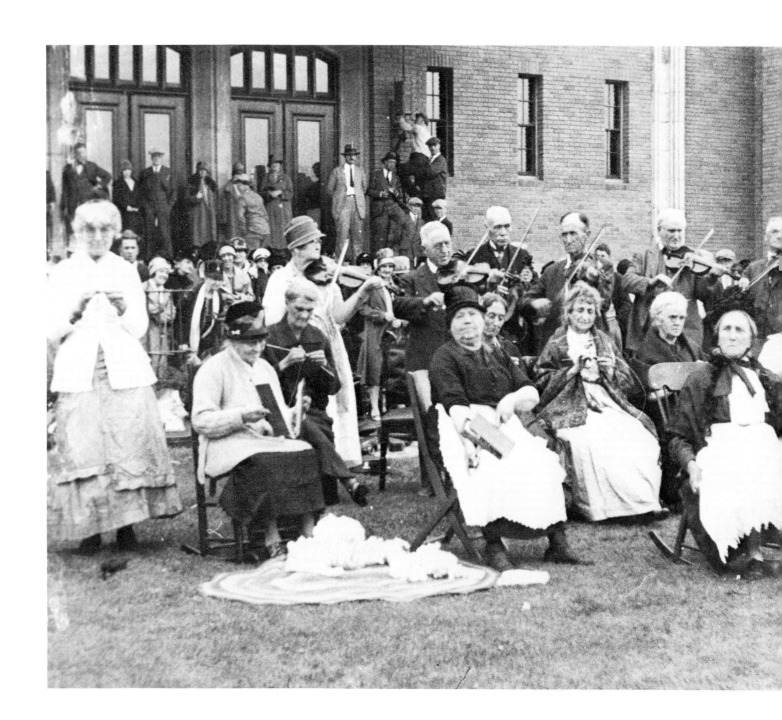

Georgia field-hands sing
spirituals, 1928.

Ukulele, washboard and kazoo, 1928.

Cuban student band, Havana, 1929.

Whistler's Jug Band, Louisville, Ky. 1930.

Some musical oddities. *Left:* "Sam Bennett of Ilmington, England preparing tunes he will come to America to teach Henry Ford." 1928. *Right:* "Father and daughter vaudeville team. Dad plays trombone upside down while daughter tap-dances." 1938. *Center below:* An all-girl jazz band, c. 1924. *Below:* Hott jazz on "water skis." Catalina Island, California, c. 1924.

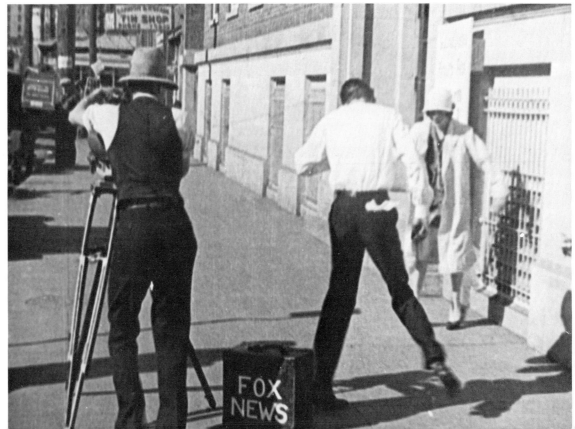

Dance to the music: *Left:* The Charleston sweeps the country, 1925.
Below: The art student's costume ball, c. 1949.

Jack Curley's Golden Slipper marathon dance contest, New York, c. 1933.

"The world's greatest Charleston dance contest." Chicago, 1925.

"Shaggers and Lindy Hoppers at the Harvest Moon Ball, with radio personality Ed Sullivan and Artie Shaw and his Orchestra." 1938. *Below:* "Jitterbug Frolic at the Harvest Moon Ball in New York with Milton Berle." 1946.

Beauty contest, Brooklyn, New York, c. 1926.

One of the first Miss America
contests: Atlantic City, New Jersey,
c. 1920.

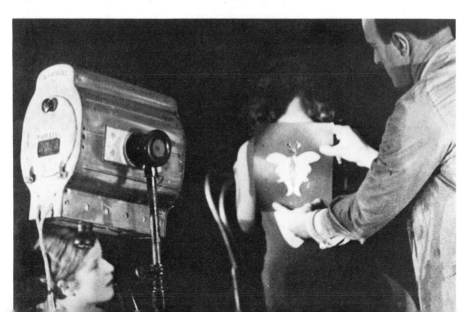

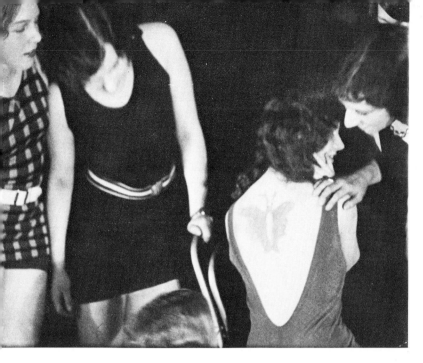

The 1920's produced a host of memorable fads. One of the dumbest appeared early in the decade: tattoo by heat lamp. Fortunately, decorative sunburn never really caught on.

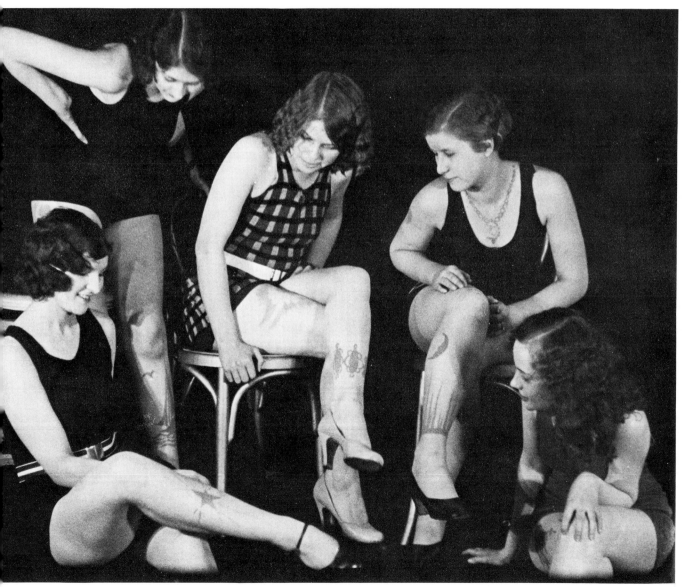

Below: "A matching ensemble. Dog, automobile and clothing."
c. 1923. *Above right:* "Young women with bangs cut in the shape
of their boyfriend's initial." 1920. *Below right:* Unliberated
women of the '20's model dog-collar garters.

Above: A 1940's fad—paddle ball. *Below:* A 1950's college fad, competitive piano destruction.

"Kids in Cleveland have a big blow-out" in a 1947 bubble-gum
blowing contest.

Above: "For the businessman in a hurry." 1924. *Below:* Motorized
chariot race by Chicago policemen, 1936.

A strong-man shows off for the cameras.
New York State, c. 1928.

Above: "Town Postmaster saves twine for 5 years to make largest
ball in the world—60 miles of string, 170 lbs. Elmhurst,
Illinois." 1925. *Below:* "Four people in Texas fat-man's trousers.
He weighs in at 696 lbs." c. 1923.

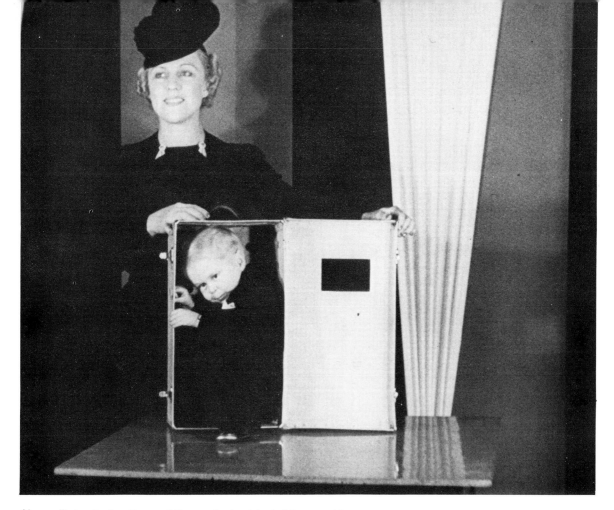

Above: "Introducing the world's smallest midget. 18-year-old
Baron Nowak is only 19 inches short, but still a hit with the
girls." 1940. *Below:* "Al Smith meets Robert Wadlow, tallest boy in
the world, 8'7", atop the Empire State Building," 1936.

The hula-hoop sweeps the world in 1962. *Below:* Frankfurt, Germany.
Above left: Detroit Michigan. *Below left:* San Diego, California (the zoo).

Left: Columbia University scholars in a 1923 mud-wrestling contest. *Below:* The Movietone film editors occasionally had fun and treated the audience to special effects. In this case, Times Square is deluged by the film "The River."

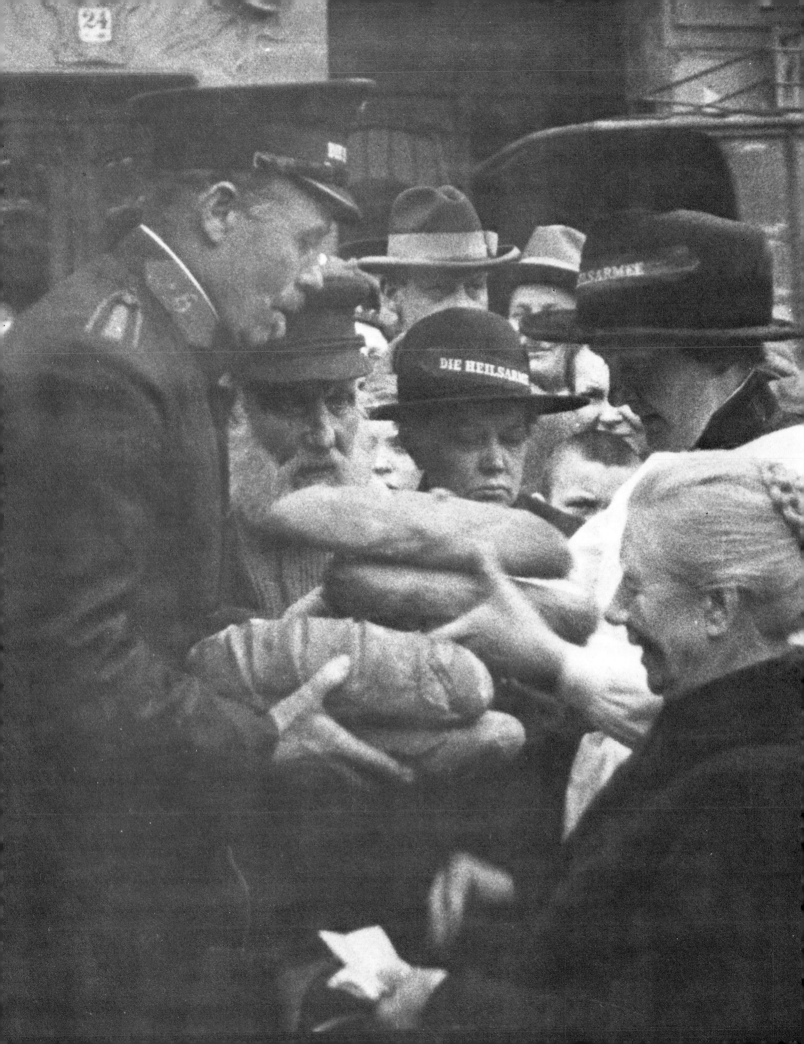

THE GREAT NEWS STORIES

From the most banal of events to those of international, far-reaching significance, the ever-present cameras of Movietone were in attendance to record for posterity countless Twentieth-Century occurrences. Coronations, disasters, new inventions, assassinations, inaugurations, weddings, foreign events and politics throughout the world were some of the subject headings that were found within this category. Exhibiting a most intrepid and aggressive approach to getting a story, Movietone's editors and cameramen were both resourceful and daring; in many cases, their activities bordered upon lunacy. They climbed the unfinished structure of the George Washington Bridge to achieve "under construction" footage, and despite being literally frozen with fear hundreds of feet up, they got the story. Famed Russell Muth flew over the mouth of an erupting volcano, shot the film, and then crashed into the side of the mountain; he walked away with a broken arm *and* his story. The tales are legion, all pointing to the dedication and resolve with which the stories were achieved.

Some important names in this area include Harry Lawrenson, Arthur DeTitta, Robert Hartmann, Fred Fresnau, and the famed Mejat brothers.

Two views of the Ku Klux Klan. *Below:* A parade in Washington, D.C. (1925), and "on the march near Atlanta, Georgia, the robed and hooded order holds an initiation ritual, as the South is aroused by latest outbreaks of the K.K.K." (1949).

These views — the only ones in existence of this mysterious Order — show an actual initiation ceremony of a "Recruit" in the woods of Stone Mountain, Ga.

Fox News

These extremely rare films of a Klan initiation were shot in 1923. Though some early Movietone sequences contained staged material, these are authentic photographs.

One of the hottest news stories of the 1920's, the Scopes "Monkey Trial," pitted two of America's greatest orators. *Above left:* John T. Scopes and Clarence Darrow. *Below left:* William Jennings Bryan. The trial dragged through the sweltering July days of 1925. Five days after the trial, Bryan was dead.

Despite occasional anti-Prohibition rallies (*left:* Boston, early 1920's), the government held to its "dry" policy throughout the '20's. Much good liquor (and much which was bad) was seized and destroyed during the noble "experiment."

G-men in action. *Above* and *Center:* Federal agents destroy a moonshine still, 1925. *Below:* Border guards seize bootleg liquor, Texas, 1926.

A staged newsreel depicting the meaning of "bootlegging."

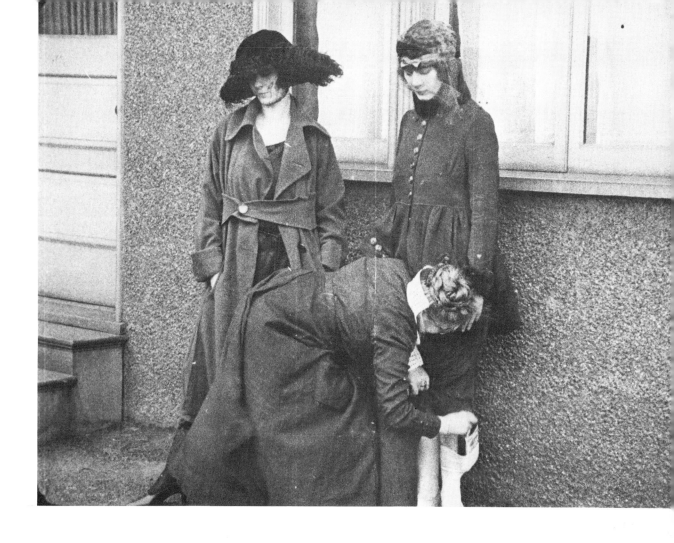

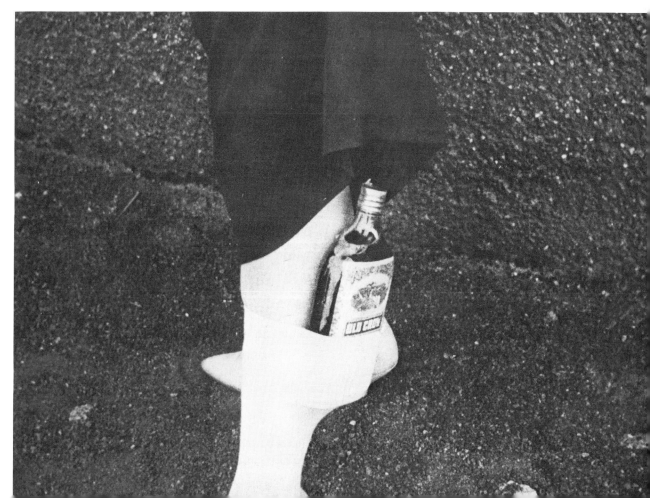

Radical labor on the march. *Above:* "Violence starts in textile strike as Roosevelt acts. 300,000 mill workers quit in South." 1934. *Left and above right:* A Socialist demonstration in Chicago, c. 1923. *Right:* The children (perhaps) of the demonstrators of the 'twenties. Communist march in New York, 1946.

The newsreel cameras covered a great many strikes and demonstrations; in this case the National Guard is called out to keep the peace during a 1925 coal strike in West Virginia.

A strike in the West Virginia coal fields, c. 1925. The miners
were evicted from company-owned housing and forced to live in tents.

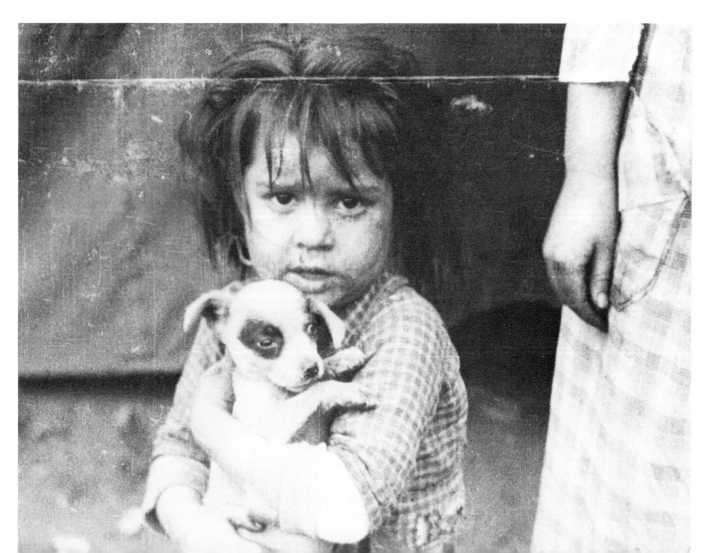

Above: "Oil discovered in Texas and comes from everywhere, even water pumps." c. 1920. *Left:* An oil fire in the East Texas fields, c. 1929. A great many of the newsreels showed on-the-spot coverage of the disaster of the week—fires, floods, earthquakes, volcanic eruptions, etc.—accompanied by ominous music and dramatic narration.

Following World War I, Germany was plunged into a
severe depression, followed by widespread hunger and
a devastating inflation. These photographs are of a
Berlin soup kitchen and bread line, 1920.

Movietone paid little attention to the beginnings of Nazism in
Germany, but neither did most newspapers until Hitler came to
power in 1933. These photos are of an early Nazi demonstration
in Berlin, c. 1925.

One of the most controversial trials of the century, the
Sacco-Vanzetti case inspired mass demonstrations around the world.
1927.

In 1932, 15,000 unemployed World War I veterans formed the "Bonus Expeditionary Force" and marched to Washington to demand payment of a bonus that had been promised them for their war service. *Above:* Under orders from President Hoover, troops led by Douglas MacArthur forcibly evicted the marchers from their makeshift quarters.

"San Francisco cops have battle with dock strikers. Tear gas bombs
are used to clear city streets of rioting stevedores." 1933.

The Hollywood Restaurant, New York City. "Hollywood Follies" with Clair Carter and the Broadway Musketeers. Even as the Depression deepened, elaborate nightclub acts were common—for those who could afford to see them.

An American tragedy and *the* trial of the decade,
the Lindbergh kidnapping case. *Above left:* Lowell
Thomas covers the trial. *Above:* Colonel Lindbergh
on the witness stand, leaving the courthouse and as a
spectator. *Opposite:* Defendant Bruno Hauptmann.
1934.

One of the most dramatic newsreel sequences of the decade. "Yugoslav king assassinated; war feared. Killing of Alexander and Foreign Minister Barthou of France at Marseilles attracts attention of the world." 1934.

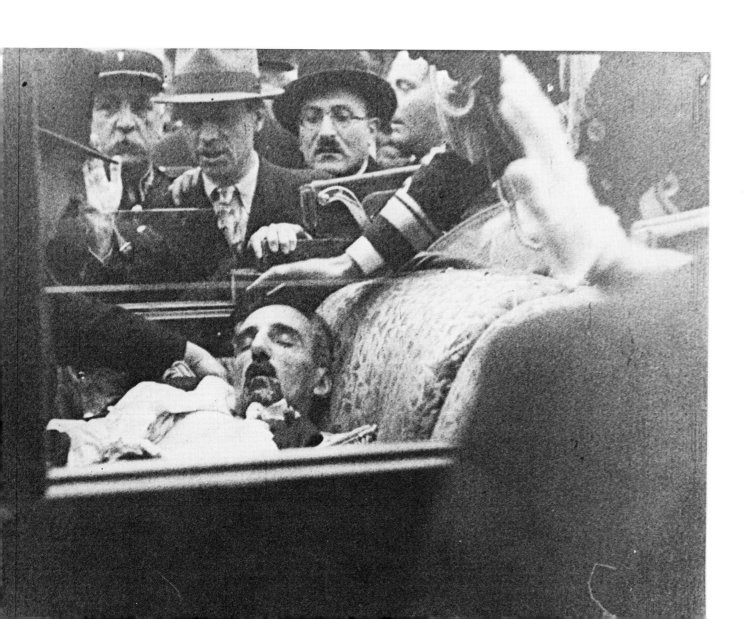

"First films of new riots in India. Exclusive pictures revealing the serious situation in Bombay as the great Hindu revolt against British rule continues." 1930.

Above left and right: "Jewish extremists sentenced; Haifa scene of tension. Barbed wire protects court where trial of terrorists held." 1946. *Below left:* "The refugee ship 'Exodus.'" 1947. *Right:* "Jewish state proclaimed at Tel Aviv. In adjoining seaport city of Jaffa, Jewish forces are in command." 1948.

"The Coronation of Queen Elizabeth. One of the greatest achievements of newsreel reportage in history with every highlight of the going and coming between Buckingham Palace and Westminster Abbey. While from the Abbey itself the cameras bring a complete drama of all the rites attending the actual crowning of Queen Elizabeth" 1953.

"England's new ruler wins the hearts of her subjects!" The coronation of Queen Elizabeth II in 1952 was one of the greatest news stories of the decade. *Above far left:* Churchill in full regalia attends the ceremony. *Below far left:* The Princess Royal, Queen Mother, Princess Margaret and a little Prince Charles receive the cheers of the crowd.

Above: Pancho Villa's troops. Mexico, c. 1921. *Below:* "Arson,
pillage and murder in Bogota Communist riot." 1950.

Displaying fiesta enthusiasm, a million Havanans turn out to hear
announcement that Dr. Fidel Castro will resume the premiership of
Cuba. 1959.

"250,000 West Berliners stage a vast patriotic rally before city hall as East German forces continue to erect blockades and barbed wire barricades at the Brandenburg Gate." 1961. *Opposite page:* "The Berlin Wall. Reds erect barricades to halt the fleeing populace. But barbed wire and check points still do not stem the tide." 1962.

Civil rights demonstrations were
among the last national movements
covered in depth by the Movietone
organization. From the mid-1950's
until operations ceased in 1963,
their cameras were on the scene at
Little Rock, Selma, New York,
Washington and elsewhere.

"The March on Washington, D.C. The Lincoln Memorial becomes the shrine to which over 200,000 pilgrims direct their steps. The Negro march on Washington had no central point on the compass, they arrived by every means of transportation. The demonstration moved to the Lincoln Memorial where they heard Martin Luther King speak, 'I Have A Dream,' along with other leaders." 1963.

SPORTS

Although handicapped by not being able to film certain important sporting events such as boxing matches, the Movietone news desk functioned largely as a visual newspaper covering all of the world's major sports and a plethora of less popular sports. It was not unusual for a single filmed report to furnish coverage of such New Year's football classics as the Rose Bowl, the Cotton Bowl and the Sugar Bowl, along with jai alai matches in Florida, and skiing at Sun Valley. Another reel might present Knute Rockne and the Notre Dame football team in spring training, the amateur ice hockey world championship in Czechoslovakia and a sailboat regatta in Australia.

Ed Thorgersen, Tom Cummiskey, Mel Allen and Paul Douglas were just some of the reporters and commentators associated with Movietone sports coverage and were by and large the most knowledgeable and widely respected names in the field.

Early motor-car races and games. 1919 and 1921.

The man who built a team which built a University, the great Knute
Rockne and the "Fighting Irish" of Notre Dame. c. 1921.

Left: Baseball's greatest, Babe Ruth, in 1919 before he was
traded to the Yankees. *Above:* Babe Ruth and Ty Cobb. c. 1925.
Below: Babe Ruth and Connie Mack in Japan with an "All-American"
baseball team. 1934.

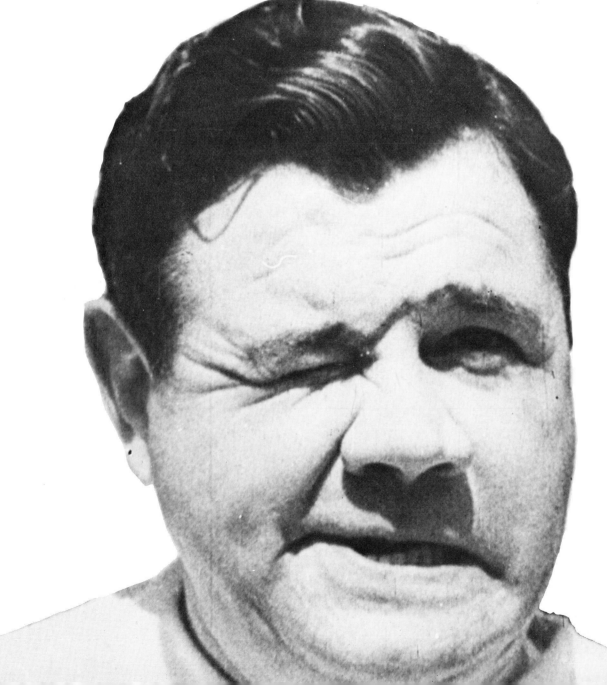

Above left: "In the most dramatic and colorful ceremonies ever to be staged on a baseball diamond, 62,000 fans and celebrities pay homage to Lou Gehrig, seen here with Babe Ruth, in testimonial to one of the games greatest stars of all time. In tears, the popular Iron Horse says 'Today I am the luckiest man on the face of the earth.'" 1939. *Below left:* Babe Ruth in 1935. *Below:* "Lou Gehrig celebrates his 2000th straight major league baseball game." 1939.

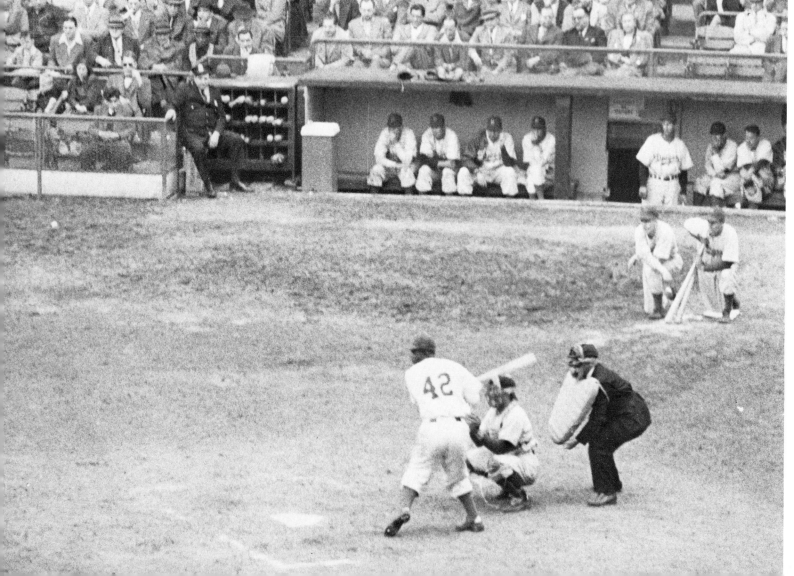

The first black man to play in the major leagues, Jackie Robinson. 1947.

"Mr. MacArthur at ball game. The General, in civvies for the first time in 11 years, gets ovation at N.Y. Polo Grounds while shaking hands with New York Giants manager Leo Durocher." 1951.

"Joe DiMaggio turns in 'No. 5'. Opening Day fans at Yankee
Stadium witness Yankee Clipper present uniform to Baseball Hall
of Fame." 1952.

Left: Probably the greatest woman athlete of all time, Babe
Didrikson. Whether in track, golf or even baseball ,
she always excelled. c. 1929. *Below:* One of the greatest pitchers
of all time, Cleveland's Bob Feller unleashes a fastball. c. 1954.

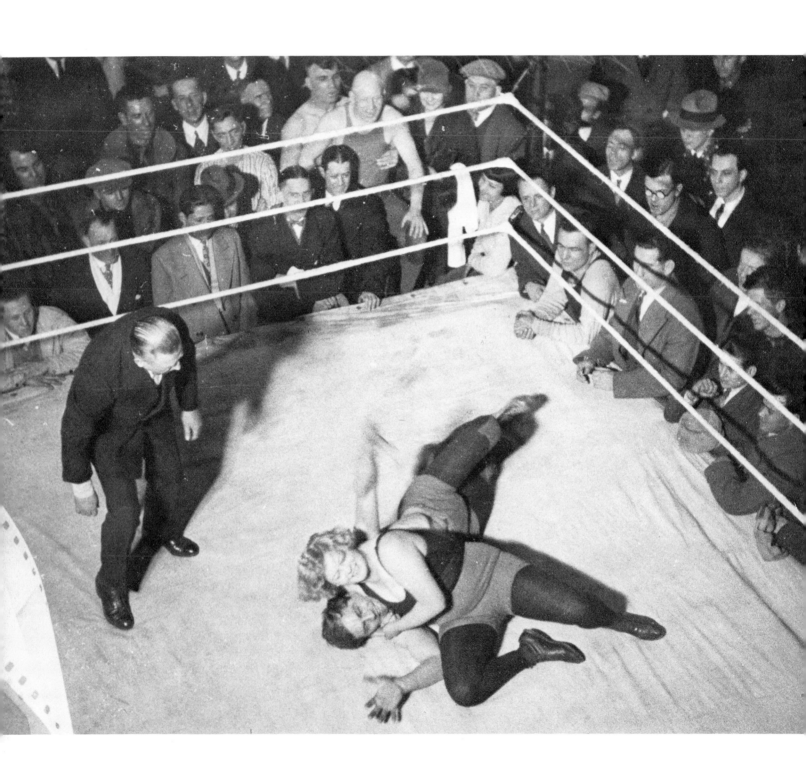

Left: Lady-wrestling was popular in the 'twenties and 'thirties.
In this shot, a woman wrestles a man . . . and wins. c. 1923. *Below:*
"The grunt and groan racket is rough on women, weak ones, that is.
Mildred Burke, in white, is still champ." 1948.

In the 1920's and 1930's boxing was a very popular sport and champions were international celebrities. This page, *top left:* GeneTunney, 1927. *Top right:* Jack Dempsey in training spars vigorously. *Above left:* The fearsome Primo Carnera, c. 1930. *Above right:* An unmussed Dempsey after a workout. 1927.

Opposite page, *above left:* Luis Firpo shows his strength. *Above right:* Primo Carnera about to clobber his sparring partner. 1930. *Opposite:* Dempsey. 1928.

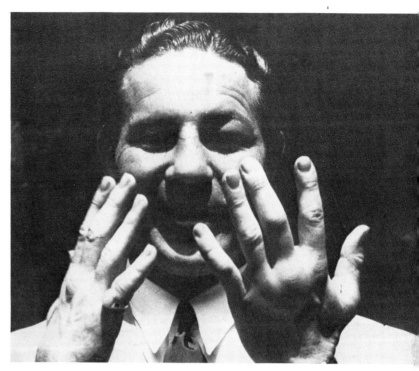

Opposite page, the great Joe Louis. *Above left:* Louis (center) and his manager, Chappie Blackburn (left) are entertained by Bill "Bojangles" Robinson. 1934. *Above right:* Louis and German fighter Max Schmeling sign for their first fight, 1937.

This page, *above left:* At his training camp, Tony Galento shows the secret of his strength—beer. 1939. *Above right:* Max Baer shows the results of a hard-fought victory. 1935. *Below:* Jersey Joe Walcott weighing in, c. 1952.

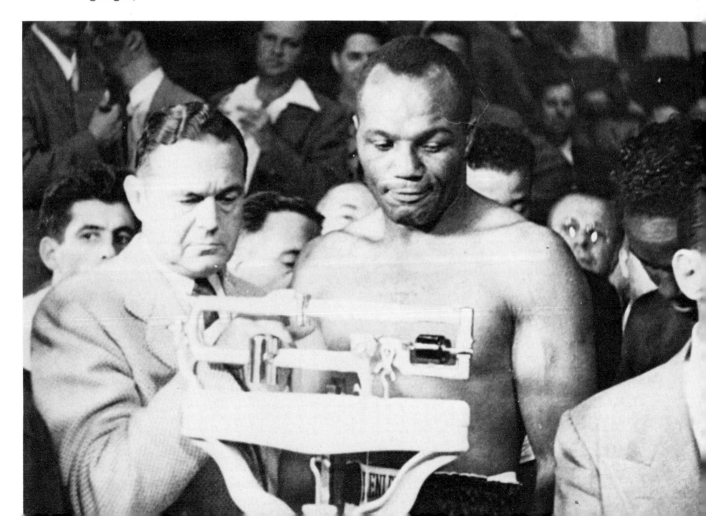

Above: "Ray Robinson and the man who held his title for a while, England's Randy Turpin." 1952. *Below:* "Rocky Graziano gets into shape for title go with Sugar Ray Robinson." 1952.

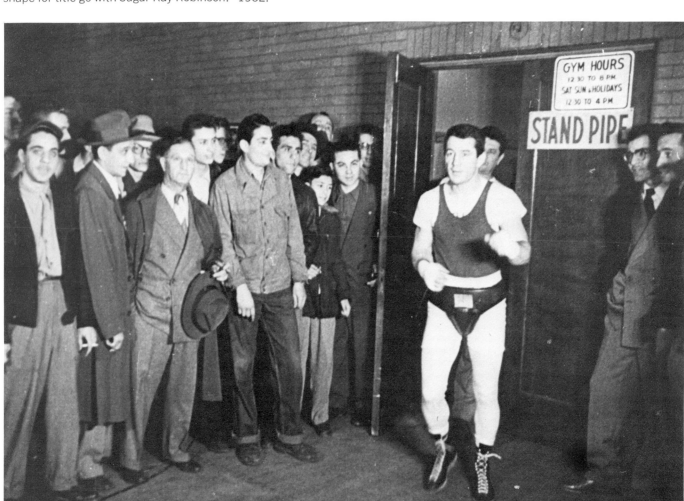

Above: "In Buenos Aires, Argentina, World Light-Heavyweight
Champion Archie Moore meets Rinaldo Ansaloni. President Peron
looks on as Moore easily outclasses the Argentinian." 1953.
Below: Sugar Ray Robinson. 1953.

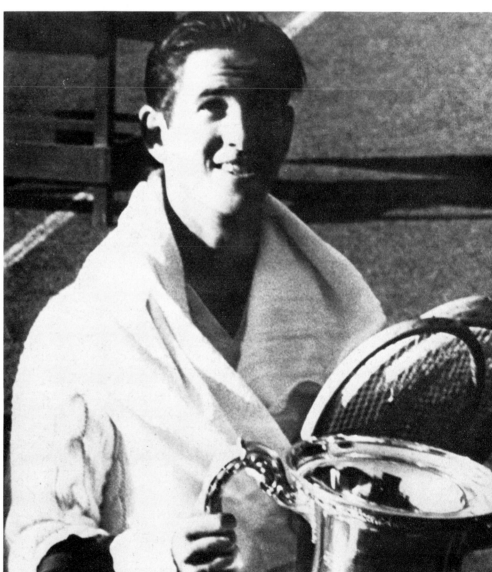

Above left: "Queen Helen Wills gives a rhythmic exhibition of tennis wizardry." 1936. *Above:* A boyish Bobby Riggs, c. 1940. Right: Certainly the greatest tennis player of the twenties, and perhaps the greatest of all time, Big Bill Tilden wins again. 1923.

Left: American women train for the 1924 Olympics. *Below:* Movietone cameras followed Gertrude Ederle as she swam the English Channel in 1926. The first woman ever to complete the grueling swim, she is shown here immediately after its completion .

"Queen's husband plays cricket. Some 30,000 look on as the Duke of Norfolk clashes with the Duke of Edinburgh in a friendly game of cricket in England." 1953.

Below: "Bantam Ben Hogan smashes the ball straight down the fairway." c. 1953.

In recent years, the Olympics have been criticized for having become too "political." It is therefore worth remembering the 1936 Olympics held in Berlin. *Below:* The opening ceremonies. *Above right:* Armed Nazi paratroopers in full uniform about to perform a platform dive (no medals were awarded for this particular event). *Below right:* Goering and Goebbels observing the games.

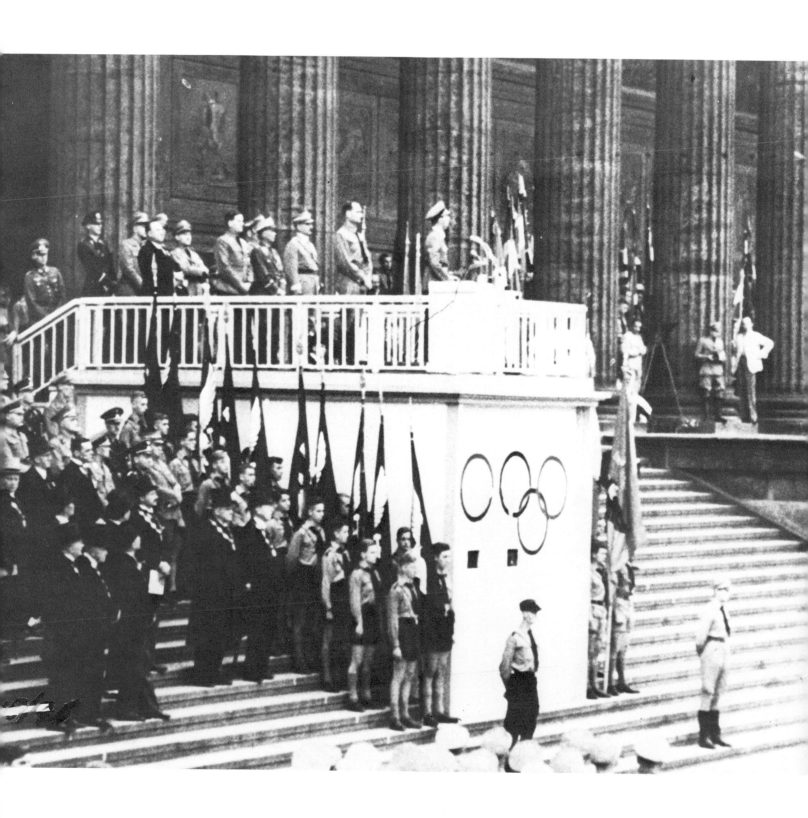

"Olympic track-star Jesse Owens and his wife return from the Berlin Olympics and are greeted by Bill "Bojangles" Robinson and Jack Dempsey." 1936.

Left: "The Reverend Bob Richards clears the fifteen-foot pole vault mark." 1952. *Below:* England's Roger Bannister does the "impossible" and runs the four-minute mile with a time of 3:59.4. Movietone cameras catch him at the moment he crosses the line. 1954.

"The year's outstanding thoroughbred, Whirlaway, again comes from behind to take the Dwyer Stakes at Aqueduct track, Eddie Arcaro the rider." 1941.

The Movietone camera boat was almost swamped when filming this speedboat race in Florida in 1953.

MARVELS
OF TECHNOLOGY

The technical achievements of this century have been both formidable and magnificent. The cameras recorded the building of dams and bridges, every permutation of advancement conceivable in aviation as well as other modes of transportation, the erection of skyscrapers, the construction of huge ocean liners, and many other marvels in an endless list of accomplishments. Fortunately, much in this area was filmed by Movietone on a worldwide basis, and the historical perspective provided parallels the advancement of Twentieth-Century man. Included in this film history are the first flight by the Wright Brothers, various record-breaking performances by Howard Hughes and Amelia Earhart, and the construction of some of the greatest bridges, skyscrapers, and monuments in history. Once again the daring of those associated with Movietone resulted in extraordinary footage, and the visual record of those myriad achievements is unequalled in newsreel reporting.

Two of the daredevil cameramen responsible for much of the aviation footage were Jack Kuhne and Larry Kennedy, with many of the other staff men contributing in all areas of technological coverage.

Extremely rare footage from the Movietone archives of the Wright brothers' first flight. Kitty Hawk, North Carolina, 1903.

"How to build an airplane." An American aircraft factory in
mass production, 1926.

The hero of the 1920's, Charles
Lindbergh. *Above:* Shortly before
his takeoff in the "Spirit of
St. Louis," 1927. *Left:* Arrival
in Paris. *Right:* Lindbergh is
honored in Los Angeles, 1928.

The heyday of the dirigible. *Left:* The British zeppelin R101, seized from the Germans after World War I. *Below:* The U.S. airship Shenandoah crashes, 1925.

The huge air ships dwarfed their human cargo. *Right:* The
Graf Zeppelin with Dr. Hugo Eckner, acknowledged genius of
lighter-than-air craft. c. 1927.

The greatest dirigible of its time. *Below:* "Movietone flies on 'Hindenburg,' giant dirigible." 1936. *Below right:* The passenger lounge.

The Hindenburg over New York City on its way to Lakehurst, New Jersey. 1937.

"Dirigible Hindenburg explodes. 50 lives lost. Giant airship plunges to earth in flames. Movietone News presents actual scenes of the most appalling tragedy in the history of lighter-than-air craft. At the end of the first transatlantic crossing of the season the great German dirigible, nosing to its mooring mast at Lakehurst, catches fire and is utterly destroyed! In one of the most spectacular scenes ever made by a motion picture camera, Movietone depicts the blinding flash of the first explosion and the horrifying plunge to earth of the flaming airship. Frantic passengers leap to the ground from a roaring inferno and in one brief minute the once proud Queen of the Air is reduced to a red-hot mass of twisted metal." 1937.

The mail must go through. In the early 1920's, a 25-hour run
from San Francisco to New York was newsworthy. *Below:* A mail
plane of the later 'twenties. *Left:* "The Lawson, America's largest
aircraft." c. 1927.

In 1922, the well-dressed airline passenger wore a parachute . . .
just in case. Weight was a critical matter since it was essential
to have sufficient fuel for long-range flights. Even with a load
of slim passengers, a flight of any great distance involved
numerous landings for re-fueling.

The evolution of the helicopter. *Left:* A "Bat-plane." c. 1929. *Below left:* "Amelia Earhart flies autogiro. Airwoman makes 18,500 feet at Philadelphia in first attempt for altitude in a wind-mill plane." *Below:* "A new air machine goes up, straight up, and lands straight down. The Sikorsky helicopter makes tests." 1940.

Above: The flying-boat Dornier *DO-X,* largest aircraft in the world. 1929. *Below:* Piggy-back aircraft. 1942. *Right:* By the late 1950's, speed, range and size no longer were problems.

Up, up and almost away. *Right:* The first (and last) flying bicycle. France, 1920. *Left:* Who needs propellers? A sail plane, Spain, 1930. *Below left:* Loading a jet-propelled bicycle, France, 1949. (It crashes.) *Below:* "Over Meridian, Mississippi, endurance fliers repair and adjust engines in the sky." 1935.

"Howard Hughes smashes coast-to-coast record. Noted motion picture producer flies his own plane from Burbank, California, to Newark in 9½ hours on business." 1935. *Right:* The great aviatrix Amelia Earhart and her husband. c. 1936.

"Largest flying boat. At Los Angeles, almost set for test flight,
is $25,000,000 craft built by Howard Hughes. 'The Spruce Goose'
has 8 motors, will carry 700 passengers." 1947.

Below: "Riverboats hail Ohio deepening. From Pittsburgh to Cairo stern-wheelers celebrate completion of $125,000,000 water-way." 1929. *Above:* A Mississippi riverboat. c. 1925.

In 1923, the largest ship in the world, the "Leviathan," was launched.
Above: Workmen pose atop the massive ship's propeller.

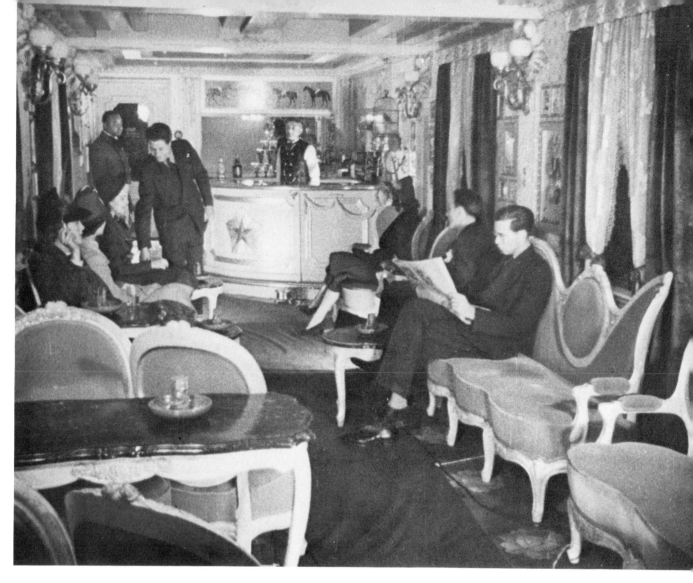

Above left: A 1920's parlor car truly resembled the parlor. *Below left:* "Largest and smallest locomotives in the world." c. 1925. *Above and below:* "A threat to the working man. Girl bell-hops service modern locomotive, c. 1927. This was most likely a publicity stunt.

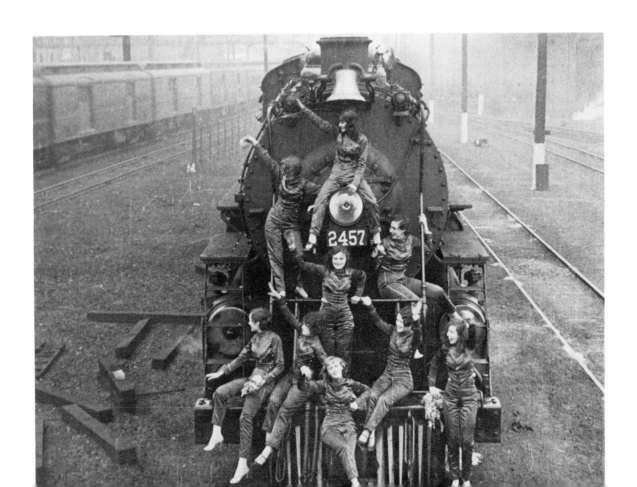

"The car of the future is here today! The 'Mars' rocket car is here seen in its first test run. Mass production is expected in the next few years." c. 1929.

Movietone cameramen took great risks on construction sites. *Above* and *below:* A skyscraper goes up in Boston in 1929. *Right:* "Seeing New York from the king of skyscrapers, 1048 feet up in the Chrysler Building, world's highest." 1929.

"A huge project near completion." Construction of the Eighth Avenue subway, 1929.

"New York City. Nerveless workmen and Movietone's cameraman dangle
in mid-air on risky job of painting new Triborough bridge." 1936.

"Giant Shasta Dam takes shape in California. Largest conveyor belt
in world transports rock 10 miles uphill for the big concrete job."
1941.

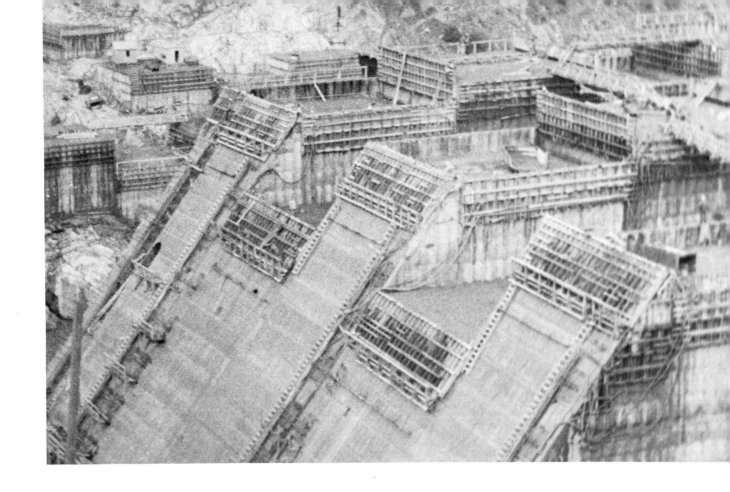

"South Dakota. Monuments in stone to Washington, Jefferson and Lincoln are near completion, carved in Mt. Rushmore." 1938. Teddy Roosevelt was added later.

MOVIETONE NEWS

NEWS